Ian Levin

THE STORY OF BEOWULF

Unknown

Published by the East India Publishing Company
Ottawa, Ontario.

© 2020 East India Publishing Company

Cover Design by EIPC. © 2020
9781774260319

Prelude

LO, praise of the prowess of people-kings
of spear-armed Danes, in days long sped,
we have heard, and what honor the athelings won!
Oft Scyld the Scefing from squadroned foes,
from many a tribe, the mead-bench tore,
awing the earls. Since erst he lay
friendless, a foundling, fate repaid him:
for he waxed under welkin, in wealth he throve,
till before him the folk, both far and near,
who house by the whale-path, heard his mandate,
gave him gifts: a good king he!
To him an heir was afterward born,
a son in his halls, whom heaven sent
to favor the folk, feeling their woe
that erst they had lacked an earl for leader
so long a while; the Lord endowed him,
the Wielder of Wonder, with world's renown.
Famed was this Beowulf:* far flew the boast of him,
son of Scyld, in the Scandian lands.
So becomes it a youth to quit him well
with his father's friends, by fee and gift,
that to aid him, aged, in after days,
come warriors willing, should war draw nigh,
liegemen loyal: by lauded deeds
shall an earl have honor in every clan.
Forth he fared at the fated moment,
sturdy Scyld to the shelter of God.
Then they bore him over to ocean's billow,
loving clansmen, as late he charged them,
while wielded words the winsome Scyld,
the leader beloved who long had ruled....
....
* Not, of course, Beowulf the Great, hero of the epic.

In the roadstead rocked a ring-dight vessel,
ice-flecked, outbound, atheling's barge:
there laid they down their darling lord
on the breast of the boat, the breaker-of-rings,*
by the mast the mighty one. Many a treasure
fetched from far was freighted with him.
No ship have I known so nobly dight
with weapons of war and weeds of battle,
with breastplate and blade: on his bosom lay
a heaped hoard that hence should go
far o'er the flood with him floating away.
No less these loaded the lordly gifts,
thanes' huge treasure, than those had done
who in former time forth had sent him
sole on the seas, a suckling child.
High o'er his head they hoist the standard,
a gold-wove banner; let billows take him,
gave him to ocean. Grave were their spirits,
mournful their mood. No man is able
to say in sooth, no son of the halls,
no hero 'neath heaven, -- who harbored that freight!

I

Now Beowulf bode in the burg of the Scyldings,
leader beloved, and long he ruled
in fame with all folk, since his father had gone
away from the world, till awoke an heir,
haughty Healfdene, who held through life,
sage and sturdy, the Scyldings glad.
Then, one after one, there woke to him,
to the chieftain of clansmen, children four:
Heorogar, then Hrothgar, then Halga brave;

....

* Kenning for king or chieftain of a comitatus: he breaks off gold
from the spiral rings -- often worn on the arm -- and so rewards
his followers.

and I heard that -- was -- 's queen,
the Heathoscylfing's helpmate dear.
To Hrothgar was given such glory of war,
such honor of combat, that all his kin
obeyed him gladly till great grew his band
of youthful comrades. It came in his mind
to bid his henchmen a hall uprear,
a master mead-house, mightier far
than ever was seen by the sons of earth,
and within it, then, to old and young
he would all allot that the Lord had sent him,
save only the land and the lives of his men.
Wide, I heard, was the work commanded,
for many a tribe this mid-earth round,
to fashion the folkstead. It fell, as he ordered,
in rapid achievement that ready it stood there,
of halls the noblest: Heorot* he named it
whose message had might in many a land.
Not reckless of promise, the rings he dealt,
treasure at banquet: there towered the hall,
high, gabled wide, the hot surge waiting

....

* That is, "The Hart," or "Stag," so called from decorations in
the gables that resembled the antlers of a deer. This hall has been
carefully described in a pamphlet by Heyne. The building was
rectangular, with opposite doors -- mainly west and east -- and
a hearth in the middle of th single room. A row of pillars down
each side, at some distance from the walls, made a space which
was raised a little above the main floor, and was furnished with
two rows of seats. On one side, usually south, was the high-seat
midway between the doors. Opposite this, on the other raised
space, was another seat of honor. At the banquet soon to be de-
scribed, Hrothgar sat in the south or chief high-seat, and Beowulf
opposite to him. The scene for a flying (see below, v.499) was thus
very effectively set. Planks on trestles -- the "board" of later En-
glish literature -- formed the tables just in front of the long rows
of seats, and were taken away after banquets, when the retainers
were ready to stretch themselves out for sleep on the benches.

of furious flame.* Nor far was that day
when father and son-in-law stood in feud
for warfare and hatred that woke again.†
With envy and anger an evil spirit
endured the dole in his dark abode,
that he heard each day the din of revel
high in the hall: there harps rang out,
clear song of the singer. He sang who knew‡
tales of the early time of man,
how the Almighty made the earth,
fairest fields enfolded by water,
set, triumphant, sun and moon
for a light to lighten the land-dwellers,
and braided bright the breast of earth
with limbs and leaves, made life for all
of mortal beings that breathe and move.
So lived the clansmen in cheer and revel
a winsome life, till one began
to fashion evils, that field of hell.
Grendel this monster grim was called,
march-riever§ mighty, in moorland living,
in fen and fastness; fief of the giants
the hapless wight a while had kept

* Fire was the usual end of these halls. See v. 781 below. One
thinks of the splendid scene at the end of the Nibelungen, of the
Nialssaga, of Saxo's story of Amlethus, and many a less famous
instance.

† It is to be supposed that all hearers of this poem knew how
Hrothgar's hall was burnt, -- perhaps in the unsuccessful attack
made on him by his son-in-law Ingeld.

‡ A skilled minstrel. The Danes are heathens, as one is told
presently; but this lay of beginnings is taken from Genesis.

§ A disturber of the border, one who sallies from his haunt in
the fen and roams over the country near by. This probably pagan
nuisance is now furnished with biblical credentials as a fiend or
devil in good standing, so that all Christian Englishmen might
read about him. "Grendel" may mean one who grinds and crush-
es.

since the Creator his exile doomed.
On kin of Cain was the killing avenged
by sovran God for slaughtered Abel.
Ill fared his feud,* and far was he driven,
for the slaughter's sake, from sight of men.
Of Cain awoke all that woful breed,
Etins† and elves and evil-spirits,
as well as the giants that warred with God
weary while: but their wage was paid them!

II

WENT he forth to find at fall of night
that haughty house, and heed wherever
the Ring-Danes, outrevelled, to rest had gone.
Found within it the atheling band
asleep after feasting and fearless of sorrow,
of human hardship. Unhallowed wight,
grim and greedy, he grasped betimes,
wrathful, reckless, from resting-places,
thirty of the thanes, and thence he rushed
fain of his fell spoil, faring homeward,
laden with slaughter, his lair to seek.
Then at the dawning, as day was breaking,
the might of Grendel to men was known;
then after wassail was wail uplifted,
loud moan in the morn. The mighty chief,
atheling excellent, unblithe sat,
labored in woe for the loss of his thanes,
when once had been traced the trail of the fiend,
spirit accurst: too cruel that sorrow,
too long, too loathsome. Not late the respite;
with night returning, anew began
ruthless murder; he recked no whit,
....
* Cain's.

† Giants.

firm in his guilt, of the feud and crime.
They were easy to find who elsewhere sought
in room remote their rest at night,
bed in the bowers,* when that bale was shown,
was seen in sooth, with surest token, --
the hall-thane's† hate. Such held themselves
far and fast who the fiend outran!
Thus ruled unrighteous and raged his fill
one against all; until empty stood
that lordly building, and long it bode so.
Twelve years' tide the trouble he bore,
sovran of Scyldings, sorrows in plenty,
boundless cares. There came unhidden
tidings true to the tribes of men,
in sorrowful songs, how ceaselessly Grendel
harassed Hrothgar, what hate he bore him,
what murder and massacre, many a year,
feud unfading, -- refused consent
to deal with any of Daneland's earls,
make pact of peace, or compound for gold:
still less did the wise men ween to get
great fee for the feud from his fiendish hands.
But the evil one ambushed old and young
death-shadow dark, and dogged them still,
lured, or lurked in the livelong night
of misty moorlands: men may say not
where the haunts of these Hell-Runes‡ be.
Such heaping of horrors the hater of men,
lonely roamer, wrought unceasing,
harassings heavy. O'er Heorot he lorded,
gold-bright hall, in gloomy nights;
and ne'er could the prince§ approach his throne,
....

* The smaller buildings within the main enclosure but separate
from the hall.

† Grendel.

‡ "Sorcerers-of-hell."

§ Hrothgar, who is the "Scyldings'-friend" of 170.

-- 'twas judgment of God, -- or have joy in his hall.
Sore was the sorrow to Scyldings'-friend,
heart-rending misery. Many nobles
sat assembled, and searched out counsel
how it were best for bold-hearted men
against harassing terror to try their hand.
Whiles they vowed in their heathen fanes
altar-offerings, asked with words*
that the slayer-of-souls would succor give them
for the pain of their people. Their practice this,
their heathen hope; 'twas Hell they thought of
in mood of their mind. Almighty they knew not,
Doomsman of Deeds and dreadful Lord,
nor Heaven's-Helmet heeded they ever,
Wielder-of-Wonder. -- Woe for that man
who in harm and hatred hales his soul
to fiery embraces; -- nor favor nor change
awaits he ever. But well for him
that after death-day may draw to his Lord,
and friendship find in the Father's arms!

III

THUS seethed unceasing the son of Healfdene
with the woe of these days; not wisest men
assuaged his sorrow; too sore the anguish,
loathly and long, that lay on his folk,
most baneful of burdens and bales of the night.
This heard in his home Hygelac's thane,
great among Geats, of Grendel's doings.
He was the mightiest man of valor
in that same day of this our life,
stalwart and stately. A stout wave-walker
he bade make ready. Yon battle-king, said he,
far o'er the swan-road he fain would seek,

....

* That is, in formal or prescribed phrase.

the noble monarch who needed men!
The prince's journey by prudent folk
was little blamed, though they loved him dear;
they whetted the hero, and hailed good omens.
And now the bold one from bands of Geats
comrades chose, the keenest of warriors
e'er he could find; with fourteen men
the sea-wood* he sought, and, sailor proved,
led them on to the land's confines.
Time had now flown; † afloat was the ship,
boat under bluff. On board they climbed,
warriors ready; waves were churning
sea with sand; the sailors bore
on the breast of the bark their bright array,
their mail and weapons: the men pushed off,
on its willing way, the well-braced craft.
Then moved o'er the waters by might of the wind
that bark like a bird with breast of foam,
till in season due, on the second day,
the curved prow such course had run
that sailors now could see the land,
sea-cliffs shining, steep high hills,
headlands broad. Their haven was found,
their journey ended. Up then quickly
the Weders'‡ clansmen climbed ashore,
anchored their sea-wood, with armor clashing
and gear of battle: God they thanked
or passing in peace o'er the paths of the sea.
Now saw from the cliff a Scylding clansman,
a warden that watched the water-side,
how they bore o'er the gangway glittering shields,
war-gear in readiness; wonder seized him
to know what manner of men they were.
....

* Ship.

† That is, since Beowulf selected his ship and led his men to the harbor.

‡ One of the auxiliary names of the Geats.

Straight to the strand his steed he rode,
Hrothgar's henchman; with hand of might
he shook his spear, and spake in parley.
"Who are ye, then, ye armed men,
mailed folk, that yon mighty vessel
have urged thus over the ocean ways,
here o'er the waters? A warden I,
sentinel set o'er the sea-march here,
lest any foe to the folk of Danes
with harrying fleet should harm the land.
No aliens ever at ease thus bore them,
linden-wielders:* yet word-of-leave
clearly ye lack from clansmen here,
my folk's agreement. -- A greater ne'er saw I
of warriors in world than is one of you, --
yon hero in harness! No henchman he
worthied by weapons, if witness his features,
his peerless presence! I pray you, though, tell
your folk and home, lest hence ye fare
suspect to wander your way as spies
in Danish land. Now, dwellers afar,
ocean-travellers, take from me
simple advice: the sooner the better
I hear of the country whence ye came."

IV

To him the stateliest spake in answer;
the warriors' leader his word-hoard unlocked: --
"We are by kin of the clan of Geats,
and Hygelac's own hearth-fellows we.
To folk afar was my father known,
noble atheling, Ecgtheow named.
Full of winters, he fared away
....
*Or: Not thus openly ever came warriors hither; yet...

aged from earth; he is honored still
through width of the world by wise men all.
To thy lord and liege in loyal mood
we hasten hither, to Healfdene's son,
people-protector: be pleased to advise us!
To that mighty-one come we on mickle errand,
to the lord of the Danes; nor deem I right
that aught be hidden. We hear -- thou knowest
if sooth it is -- the saying of men,
that amid the Scyldings a scathing monster,
dark ill-doer, in dusky nights
shows terrific his rage unmatched,
hatred and murder. To Hrothgar I
in greatness of soul would succor bring,
so the Wise-and-Brave* may worst his foes, --
if ever the end of ills is fated,
of cruel contest, if cure shall follow,
and the boiling care-waves cooler grow;
else ever afterward anguish-days
he shall suffer in sorrow while stands in place
high on its hill that house unpeered!"
Astride his steed, the strand-ward answered,
clansman unquailing: "The keen-souled thane
must be skilled to sever and sunder duly
words and works, if he well intends.
I gather, this band is graciously bent
to the Scyldings' master. March, then, bearing
weapons and weeds the way I show you.
I will bid my men your boat meanwhile
to guard for fear lest foemen come, --
your new-tarred ship by shore of ocean
faithfully watching till once again
it waft o'er the waters those well-loved thanes,
-- winding-neck'd wood, -- to Weders' bounds,
heroes such as the hest of fate

....
* Hrothgar.

shall succor and save from the shock of war."
They bent them to march, -- the boat lay still,
fettered by cable and fast at anchor,
broad-bosomed ship. -- Then shone the boars*
over the cheek-guard; chased with gold,
keen and gleaming, guard it kept
o'er the man of war, as marched along
heroes in haste, till the hall they saw,
broad of gable and bright with gold:
that was the fairest, 'mid folk of earth,
of houses 'neath heaven, where Hrothgar lived,
and the gleam of it lightened o'er lands afar.
The sturdy shieldsman showed that bright
burg-of-the-boldest; bade them go
straightway thither; his steed then turned,
hardy hero, and hailed them thus: --
"'Tis time that I fare from you. Father Almighty
in grace and mercy guard you well,
safe in your seekings. Seaward I go,
'gainst hostile warriors hold my watch."

V

STONE-BRIGHT the street:† it showed the way
to the crowd of clansmen. Corselets glistened
hand-forged, hard; on their harness bright
the steel ring sang, as they strode along
in mail of battle, and marched to the hall.

....

* Beowulf's helmet has several boar-images on it; he is the "man
of war"; and the boar-helmet guards him as typical representative
of the marching party as a whole. The boar was sacred to Freyr,
who was the favorite god of the Germanic tribes about the North
Sea and the Baltic. Rude representations of warriors show the
boar on the helmet quite as large as the helmet itself.

† Either merely paved, the strata via of the Romans, or else
thought of as a sort of mosaic, an extravagant touch like the
reckless waste of gold on the walls and roofs of a hall.

There, weary of ocean, the wall along
they set their bucklers, their broad shields, down,
and bowed them to bench: the breastplates clanged,
war-gear of men; their weapons stacked,
spears of the seafarers stood together,
gray-tipped ash: that iron band
was worthily weaponed! -- A warrior proud
asked of the heroes their home and kin.
"Whence, now, bear ye burnished shields,
harness gray and helmets grim,
spears in multitude? Messenger, I,
Hrothgar's herald! Heroes so many
ne'er met I as strangers of mood so strong.
'Tis plain that for prowess, not plunged into exile,
for high-hearted valor, Hrothgar ye seek!"
Him the sturdy-in-war bespake with words,
proud earl of the Weders answer made,
hardy 'neath helmet: -- "Hygelac's, we,
fellows at board; I am Beowulf named.
I am seeking to say to the son of Healfdene
this mission of mine, to thy master-lord,
the doughty prince, if he deign at all
grace that we greet him, the good one, now."
Wulfgar spake, the Wendles' chieftain,
whose might of mind to many was known,
his courage and counsel: "The king of Danes,
the Scyldings' friend, I fain will tell,
the Breaker-of-Rings, as the boon thou askest,
the famed prince, of thy faring hither,
and, swiftly after, such answer bring
as the doughty monarch may deign to give."
Hied then in haste to where Hrothgar sat
white-haired and old, his earls about him,
till the stout thane stood at the shoulder there
of the Danish king: good courtier he!
Wulfgar spake to his winsome lord: --
"Hither have fared to thee far-come men

o'er the paths of ocean, people of Geatland;
and the stateliest there by his sturdy band
is Beowulf named. This boon they seek,
that they, my master, may with thee
have speech at will: nor spurn their prayer
to give them hearing, gracious Hrothgar!
In weeds of the warrior worthy they,
methinks, of our liking; their leader most surely,
a hero that hither his henchmen has led."

VI

HROTHGAR answered, helmet of Scyldings: --
"I knew him of yore in his youthful days;
his aged father was Ecgtheow named,
to whom, at home, gave Hrethel the Geat
his only daughter. Their offspring bold
fares hither to seek the steadfast friend.
And seamen, too, have said me this, --
who carried my gifts to the Geatish court,
thither for thanks, -- he has thirty men's
heft of grasp in the gripe of his hand,
the bold-in-battle. Blessed God
out of his mercy this man hath sent
to Danes of the West, as I ween indeed,
against horror of Grendel. I hope to give
the good youth gold for his gallant thought.
Be thou in haste, and bid them hither,
clan of kinsmen, to come before me;
and add this word, -- they are welcome guests
to folk of the Danes."
[To the door of the hall
Wulfgar went] and the word declared: --
"To you this message my master sends,
East-Danes' king, that your kin he knows,
hardy heroes, and hails you all

welcome hither o'er waves of the sea!
Ye may wend your way in war-attire,
and under helmets Hrothgar greet;
but let here the battle-shields bide your parley,
and wooden war-shafts wait its end."
Uprose the mighty one, ringed with his men,
brave band of thanes: some bode without,
battle-gear guarding, as bade the chief.
Then hied that troop where the herald led them,
under Heorot's roof: [the hero strode,]
hardy 'neath helm, till the hearth he neared.
Beowulf spake, -- his breastplate gleamed,
war-net woven by wit of the smith: --
"Thou Hrothgar, hail! Hygelac's I,
kinsman and follower. Fame a plenty
have I gained in youth! These Grendel-deeds
I heard in my home-land heralded clear.
Seafarers say how stands this hall,
of buildings best, for your band of thanes
empty and idle, when evening sun
in the harbor of heaven is hidden away.
So my vassals advised me well, --
brave and wise, the best of men, --
O sovran Hrothgar, to seek thee here,
for my nerve and my might they knew full well.
Themselves had seen me from slaughter come
blood-flecked from foes, where five I bound,
and that wild brood worsted. I' the waves I slew
nicors* by night, in need and peril
avenging the Weders,† whose woe they sought, --
crushing the grim ones. Grendel now,
monster cruel, be mine to quell

....

* The nicor, says Bugge, is a hippopotamus; a walrus, says Ten
Brink. But that water-goblin who covers the space from Old Nick
of jest to the Neckan and Nix of poetry and tale, is all one needs,
and Nicor is a good name for him.

† His own people, the Geats.

in single battle! So, from thee,
thou sovran of the Shining-Danes,
Scyldings'-bulwark, a boon I seek, --
and, Friend-of-the-folk, refuse it not,
O Warriors'-shield, now I've wandered far, --
that I alone with my liegemen here,
this hardy band, may Heorot purge!
More I hear, that the monster dire,
in his wanton mood, of weapons recks not;
hence shall I scorn -- so Hygelac stay,
king of my kindred, kind to me! --
brand or buckler to bear in the fight,
gold-colored targe: but with gripe alone
must I front the fiend and fight for life,
foe against foe. Then faith be his
in the doom of the Lord whom death shall take.
Fain, I ween, if the fight he win,
in this hall of gold my Geatish band
will he fearless eat, -- as oft before, --
my noblest thanes. Nor need'st thou then
to hide my head;* for his shall I be,
dyed in gore, if death must take me;
and my blood-covered body he'll bear as prey,
ruthless devour it, the roamer-lonely,
with my life-blood redden his lair in the fen:
no further for me need'st food prepare!
To Hygelac send, if Hild† should take me,
best of war-weeds, warding my breast,
armor excellent, heirloom of Hrethel
and work of Wayland.‡ Fares Wyrd§ as she must."

....

* That is, cover it as with a face-cloth. "There will be no need of funeral rites."

† Personification of Battle.

‡ The Germanic Vulcan.

§ This mighty power, whom the Christian poet can still revere, has here the general force of "Destiny."

VII

HROTHGAR spake, the Scyldings'-helmet: --
"For fight defensive, Friend my Beowulf,
to succor and save, thou hast sought us here.
Thy father's combat* a feud enkindled
when Heatholaf with hand he slew
among the Wylfings; his Weder kin
for horror of fighting feared to hold him.
Fleeing, he sought our South-Dane folk,
over surge of ocean the Honor-Scyldings,
when first I was ruling the folk of Danes,
wielded, youthful, this widespread realm,
this hoard-hold of heroes. Heorogar was dead,
my elder brother, had breathed his last,
Healfdene's bairn: he was better than I!
Straightway the feud with fee† I settled,
to the Wylfings sent, o'er watery ridges,
treasures olden: oaths he‡ swore me.
Sore is my soul to say to any
of the race of man what ruth for me
in Heorot Grendel with hate hath wrought,
what sudden harryings. Hall-folk fail me,
my warriors wane; for Wyrd hath swept them
into Grendel's grasp. But God is able
this deadly foe from his deeds to turn!
Boasted full oft, as my beer they drank,
earls o'er the ale-cup, armed men,
that they would bide in the beer-hall here,
Grendel's attack with terror of blades.
Then was this mead-house at morning tide
....

* There is no irrelevance here. Hrothgar sees in Beowulf's mission
a heritage of duty, a return of the good offices which the Danish
king rendered to Beowulf's father in time of dire need.

† Money, for wergild, or man-price.

‡ Ecgtheow, Beowulf's sire.

dyed with gore, when the daylight broke,
all the boards of the benches blood-besprinkled,
gory the hall: I had heroes the less,
doughty dear-ones that death had reft.
-- But sit to the banquet, unbind thy words,
hardy hero, as heart shall prompt thee."
Gathered together, the Geatish men
in the banquet-hall on bench assigned,
sturdy-spirited, sat them down,
hardy-hearted. A henchman attended,
carried the carven cup in hand,
served the clear mead. Oft minstrels sang
blithe in Heorot. Heroes revelled,
no dearth of warriors, Weder and Dane.

VIII

UNFERTH spake, the son of Ecglaf,
who sat at the feet of the Scyldings' lord,
unbound the battle-runes.* -- Beowulf's quest,
sturdy seafarer's, sorely galled him;
ever he envied that other men
should more achieve in middle-earth
of fame under heaven than he himself. --
"Art thou that Beowulf, Breca's rival,
who emulous swam on the open sea,
when for pride the pair of you proved the floods,
and wantonly dared in waters deep
to risk your lives? No living man,
or lief or loath, from your labor dire
could you dissuade, from swimming the main.
Ocean-tides with your arms ye covered,
with strenuous hands the sea-streets measured,
swam o'er the waters. Winter's storm
rolled the rough waves. In realm of sea
....
* "Began the fight."

a sennight strove ye. In swimming he topped thee,
had more of main! Him at morning-tide
billows bore to the Battling Reamas,
whence he hied to his home so dear
beloved of his liegemen, to land of Brondings,
fastness fair, where his folk he ruled,
town and treasure. In triumph o'er thee
Beanstan's bairn* his boast achieved.
So ween I for thee a worse adventure
-- though in buffet of battle thou brave hast been,
in struggle grim, -- if Grendel's approach
thou darst await through the watch of night!"
Beowulf spake, bairn of Ecgtheow: --
"What a deal hast uttered, dear my Unferth,
drunken with beer, of Breca now,
told of his triumph! Truth I claim it,
that I had more of might in the sea
than any man else, more ocean-endurance.
We twain had talked, in time of youth,
and made our boast, -- we were merely boys,
striplings still, -- to stake our lives
far at sea: and so we performed it.
Naked swords, as we swam along,
we held in hand, with hope to guard us
against the whales. Not a whit from me
could he float afar o'er the flood of waves,
haste o'er the billows; nor him I abandoned.
Together we twain on the tides abode
five nights full till the flood divided us,
churning waves and chillest weather,
darkling night, and the northern wind
ruthless rushed on us: rough was the surge.
Now the wrath of the sea-fish rose apace;
yet me 'gainst the monsters my mailed coat,
hard and hand-linked, help afforded, --
battle-sark braided my breast to ward,

....
* Breca.

garnished with gold. There grasped me firm
and haled me to bottom the hated foe,
with grimmest gripe. 'Twas granted me, though,
to pierce the monster with point of sword,
with blade of battle: huge beast of the sea
was whelmed by the hurly through hand of mine.

IX

ME thus often the evil monsters
thronging threatened. With thrust of my sword,
the darling, I dealt them due return!
Nowise had they bliss from their booty then
to devour their victim, vengeful creatures,
seated to banquet at bottom of sea;
but at break of day, by my brand sore hurt,
on the edge of ocean up they lay,
put to sleep by the sword. And since, by them
on the fathomless sea-ways sailor-folk
are never molested. -- Light from east,
came bright God's beacon; the billows sank,
so that I saw the sea-cliffs high,
windy walls. For Wyrd oft saveth
earl undoomed if he doughty be!
And so it came that I killed with my sword
nine of the nicors. Of night-fought battles
ne'er heard I a harder 'neath heaven's dome,
nor adrift on the deep a more desolate man!
Yet I came unharmed from that hostile clutch,
though spent with swimming. The sea upbore me,
flood of the tide, on Finnish land,
the welling waters. No wise of thee
have I heard men tell such terror of falchions,
bitter battle. Breca ne'er yet,
not one of you pair, in the play of war
such daring deed has done at all

with bloody brand, -- I boast not of it! --
though thou wast the bane* of thy brethren dear,
thy closest kin, whence curse of hell
awaits thee, well as thy wit may serve!
For I say in sooth, thou son of Ecglaf,
never had Grendel these grim deeds wrought,
monster dire, on thy master dear,
in Heorot such havoc, if heart of thine
were as battle-bold as thy boast is loud!
But he has found no feud will happen;
from sword-clash dread of your Danish clan
he vaunts him safe, from the Victor-Scyldings.
He forces pledges, favors none
of the land of Danes, but lustily murders,
fights and feasts, nor feud he dreads
from Spear-Dane men. But speedily now
shall I prove him the prowess and pride of the Geats,
shall bid him battle. Blithe to mead
go he that listeth, when light of dawn
this morrow morning o'er men of earth,
ether-robed sun from the south shall beam!"
Joyous then was the Jewel-giver,
hoar-haired, war-brave; help awaited
the Bright-Danes' prince, from Beowulf hearing,
folk's good shepherd, such firm resolve.
Then was laughter of liegemen loud resounding
with winsome words. Came Wealhtheow forth,
queen of Hrothgar, heedful of courtesy,
gold-decked, greeting the guests in hall;
and the high-born lady handed the cup
first to the East-Danes' heir and warden,
bade him be blithe at the beer-carouse,
the land's beloved one. Lustily took he
banquet and beaker, battle-famed king.
Through the hall then went the Helmings' Lady,
to younger and older everywhere

....
* Murder.

carried the cup, till come the moment
when the ring-graced queen, the royal-hearted,
to Beowulf bore the beaker of mead.
She greeted the Geats' lord, God she thanked,
in wisdom's words, that her will was granted,
that at last on a hero her hope could lean
for comfort in terrors. The cup he took,
hardy-in-war, from Wealhtheow's hand,
and answer uttered the eager-for-combat.
Beowulf spake, bairn of Ecgtheow: --
"This was my thought, when my thanes and I
bent to the ocean and entered our boat,
that I would work the will of your people
fully, or fighting fall in death,
in fiend's gripe fast. I am firm to do
an earl's brave deed, or end the days
of this life of mine in the mead-hall here."
Well these words to the woman seemed,
Beowulf's battle-boast. -- Bright with gold
the stately dame by her spouse sat down.
Again, as erst, began in hall
warriors' wassail and words of power,
the proud-band's revel, till presently
the son of Healfdene hastened to seek
rest for the night; he knew there waited
fight for the fiend in that festal hall,
when the sheen of the sun they saw no more,
and dusk of night sank darkling nigh,
and shadowy shapes came striding on,
wan under welkin. The warriors rose.
Man to man, he made harangue,
Hrothgar to Beowulf, bade him hail,
let him wield the wine hall: a word he added: --
"Never to any man erst I trusted,
since I could heave up hand and shield,
this noble Dane-Hall, till now to thee.
Have now and hold this house unpeered;

remember thy glory; thy might declare;
watch for the foe! No wish shall fail thee
if thou bidest the battle with bold-won life."

X

THEN Hrothgar went with his hero-train,
defence-of-Scyldings, forth from hall;
fain would the war-lord Wealhtheow seek,
couch of his queen. The King-of-Glory
against this Grendel a guard had set,
so heroes heard, a hall-defender,
who warded the monarch and watched for the monster.
In truth, the Geats' prince gladly trusted
his mettle, his might, the mercy of God!
Cast off then his corselet of iron,
helmet from head; to his henchman gave, --
choicest of weapons, -- the well-chased sword,
bidding him guard the gear of battle.
Spake then his Vaunt the valiant man,
Beowulf Geat, ere the bed be sought: --
"Of force in fight no feebler I count me,
in grim war-deeds, than Grendel deems him.
Not with the sword, then, to sleep of death
his life will I give, though it lie in my power.
No skill is his to strike against me,
my shield to hew though he hardy be,
bold in battle; we both, this night,
shall spurn the sword, if he seek me here,
unweaponed, for war. Let wisest God,
sacred Lord, on which side soever
doom decree as he deemeth right."
Reclined then the chieftain, and cheek-pillows held
the head of the earl, while all about him
seamen hardy on hall-beds sank.
None of them thought that thence their steps

to the folk and fastness that fostered them,
to the land they loved, would lead them back!
Full well they wist that on warriors many
battle-death seized, in the banquet-hall,
of Danish clan. But comfort and help,
war-weal weaving, to Weder folk
the Master gave, that, by might of one,
over their enemy all prevailed,
by single strength. In sooth 'tis told
that highest God o'er human kind
hath wielded ever! -- Thro' wan night striding,
came the walker-in-shadow. Warriors slept
whose hest was to guard the gabled hall, --
all save one. 'Twas widely known
that against God's will the ghostly ravager
him* could not hurl to haunts of darkness;
wakeful, ready, with warrior's wrath,
bold he bided the battle's issue.

XI

THEN from the moorland, by misty crags,
with God's wrath laden, Grendel came.
The monster was minded of mankind now
sundry to seize in the stately house.
Under welkin he walked, till the wine-palace there,
gold-hall of men, he gladly discerned,
flashing with fretwork. Not first time, this,
that he the home of Hrothgar sought, --
yet ne'er in his life-day, late or early,
such hardy heroes, such hall-thanes, found!
To the house the warrior walked apace,
parted from peace;† the portal opended,
though with forged bolts fast, when his fists had
....

* Beowulf, -- the "one."

†That is, he was a "lost soul," doomed to hell.

struck it,
and baleful he burst in his blatant rage,
the house's mouth. All hastily, then,
o'er fair-paved floor the fiend trod on,
ireful he strode; there streamed from his eyes
fearful flashes, like flame to see.
He spied in hall the hero-band,
kin and clansmen clustered asleep,
hardy liegemen. Then laughed his heart;
for the monster was minded, ere morn should dawn,
savage, to sever the soul of each,
life from body, since lusty banquet
waited his will! But Wyrd forbade him
to seize any more of men on earth
after that evening. Eagerly watched
Hygelac's kinsman his cursed foe,
how he would fare in fell attack.
Not that the monster was minded to pause!
Straightway he seized a sleeping warrior
for the first, and tore him fiercely asunder,
the bone-frame bit, drank blood in streams,
swallowed him piecemeal: swiftly thus
the lifeless corse was clear devoured,
e'en feet and hands. Then farther he hied;
for the hardy hero with hand he grasped,
felt for the foe with fiendish claw,
for the hero reclining, -- who clutched it boldly,
prompt to answer, propped on his arm.
Soon then saw that shepherd-of-evils
that never he met in this middle-world,
in the ways of earth, another wight
with heavier hand-gripe; at heart he feared,
sorrowed in soul, -- none the sooner escaped!
Fain would he flee, his fastness seek,
the den of devils: no doings now
such as oft he had done in days of old!
Then bethought him the hardy Hygelac-thane

of his boast at evening: up he bounded,
grasped firm his foe, whose fingers cracked.
The fiend made off, but the earl close followed.
The monster meant -- if he might at all --
to fling himself free, and far away
fly to the fens, -- knew his fingers' power
in the gripe of the grim one. Gruesome march
to Heorot this monster of harm had made!
Din filled the room; the Danes were bereft,
castle-dwellers and clansmen all,
earls, of their ale. Angry were both
those savage hall-guards: the house resounded.
Wonder it was the wine-hall firm
in the strain of their struggle stood, to earth
the fair house fell not; too fast it was
within and without by its iron bands
craftily clamped; though there crashed from sill
many a mead-bench -- men have told me --
gay with gold, where the grim foes wrestled.
So well had weened the wisest Scyldings
that not ever at all might any man
that bone-decked, brave house break asunder,
crush by craft, -- unless clasp of fire
in smoke engulfed it. -- Again uprose
din redoubled. Danes of the North
with fear and frenzy were filled, each one,
who from the wall that wailing heard,
God's foe sounding his grisly song,
cry of the conquered, clamorous pain
from captive of hell. Too closely held him
he who of men in might was strongest
in that same day of this our life.

XII

NOT in any wise would the earls'-defence*
suffer that slaughterous stranger to live,
useless deeming his days and years
to men on earth. Now many an earl
of Beowulf brandished blade ancestral,
fain the life of their lord to shield,
their praised prince, if power were theirs;
never they knew, -- as they neared the foe,
hardy-hearted heroes of war,
aiming their swords on every side
the accursed to kill, -- no keenest blade,
no farest of falchions fashioned on earth,
could harm or hurt that hideous fiend!
He was safe, by his spells, from sword of battle,
from edge of iron. Yet his end and parting
on that same day of this our life
woful should be, and his wandering soul
far off flit to the fiends' domain.
Soon he found, who in former days,
harmful in heart and hated of God,
on many a man such murder wrought,
that the frame of his body failed him now.
For him the keen-souled kinsman of Hygelac
held in hand; hateful alive
was each to other. The outlaw dire
took mortal hurt; a mighty wound
showed on his shoulder, and sinews cracked,
and the bone-frame burst. To Beowulf now
the glory was given, and Grendel thence
death-sick his den in the dark moor sought,
noisome abode: he knew too well
that here was the last of life, an end
of his days on earth. -- To all the Danes
by that bloody battle the boon had come.
From ravage had rescued the roving stranger
Hrothgar's hall; the hardy and wise one

....
* Kenning for Beowulf.

had purged it anew. His night-work pleased him,
his deed and its honor. To Eastern Danes
had the valiant Geat his vaunt made good,
all their sorrow and ills assuaged,
their bale of battle borne so long,
and all the dole they erst endured
pain a-plenty. -- 'Twas proof of this,
when the hardy-in-fight a hand laid down,
arm and shoulder, -- all, indeed,
of Grendel's gripe, -- 'neath the gabled roof.

XIII

MANY at morning, as men have told me,
warriors gathered the gift-hall round,
folk-leaders faring from far and near,
o'er wide-stretched ways, the wonder to view,
trace of the traitor. Not troublous seemed
the enemy's end to any man
who saw by the gait of the graceless foe
how the weary-hearted, away from thence,
baffled in battle and banned, his steps
death-marked dragged to the devils' mere.
Bloody the billows were boiling there,
turbid the tide of tumbling waves
horribly seething, with sword-blood hot,
by that doomed one dyed, who in den of the moor
laid forlorn his life adown,
his heathen soul, and hell received it.
Home then rode the hoary clansmen
from that merry journey, and many a youth,
on horses white, the hardy warriors,
back from the mere. Then Beowulf's glory
eager they echoed, and all averred
that from sea to sea, or south or north,
there was no other in earth's domain,

under vault of heaven, more valiant found,
of warriors none more worthy to rule!
(On their lord beloved they laid no slight,
gracious Hrothgar: a good king he!)
From time to time, the tried-in-battle
their gray steeds set to gallop amain,
and ran a race when the road seemed fair.
From time to time, a thane of the king,
who had made many vaunts, and was mindful of verses,
stored with sagas and songs of old,
bound word to word in well-knit rime,
welded his lay; this warrior soon
of Beowulf's quest right cleverly sang,
and artfully added an excellent tale,
in well-ranged words, of the warlike deeds
he had heard in saga of Sigemund.
Strange the story: he said it all, --
the Waelsing's wanderings wide, his struggles,
which never were told to tribes of men,
the feuds and the frauds, save to Fitela only,
when of these doings he deigned to speak,
uncle to nephew; as ever the twain
stood side by side in stress of war,
and multitude of the monster kind
they had felled with their swords. Of Sigemund grew,
when he passed from life, no little praise;
for the doughty-in-combat a dragon killed
that herded the hoard:* under hoary rock
the atheling dared the deed alone
fearful quest, nor was Fitela there.
Yet so it befell, his falchion pierced
that wondrous worm, -- on the wall it struck,
best blade; the dragon died in its blood.
Thus had the dread-one by daring achieved
over the ring-hoard to rule at will,
himself to pleasure; a sea-boat he loaded,
....
* "Guarded the treasure."

and bore on its bosom the beaming gold,
son of Waels; the worm was consumed.
He had of all heroes the highest renown
among races of men, this refuge-of-warriors,
for deeds of daring that decked his name
since the hand and heart of Heremod
grew slack in battle. He, swiftly banished
to mingle with monsters at mercy of foes,
to death was betrayed; for torrents of sorrow
had lamed him too long; a load of care
to earls and athelings all he proved.
Oft indeed, in earlier days,
for the warrior's wayfaring wise men mourned,
who had hoped of him help from harm and bale,
and had thought their sovran's son would thrive,
follow his father, his folk protect,
the hoard and the stronghold, heroes' land,
home of Scyldings. -- But here, thanes said,
the kinsman of Hygelac kinder seemed
to all: the other* was urged to crime!
And afresh to the race,† the fallow roads
by swift steeds measured! The morning sun
was climbing higher. Clansmen hastened
to the high-built hall, those hardy-minded,
the wonder to witness. Warden of treasure,
crowned with glory, the king himself,
with stately band from the bride-bower strode;
and with him the queen and her crowd of maidens
measured the path to the mead-house fair.

....

* Sc. Heremod.

† The singer has sung his lays, and the epic resumes its story.
The time-relations are not altogether good in this long passage
which describes the rejoicings of "the day after"; but the present
shift from the riders on the road to the folk at the hall is not very
violent, and is of a piece with the general style.

XIV

HROTHGAR spake, -- to the hall he went,
stood by the steps, the steep roof saw,
garnished with gold, and Grendel's hand: --
"For the sight I see to the Sovran Ruler
be speedy thanks! A throng of sorrows
I have borne from Grendel; but God still works
wonder on wonder, the Warden-of-Glory.
It was but now that I never more
for woes that weighed on me waited help
long as I lived, when, laved in blood,
stood sword-gore-stained this stateliest house, --
widespread woe for wise men all,
who had no hope to hinder ever
foes infernal and fiendish sprites
from havoc in hall. This hero now,
by the Wielder's might, a work has done
that not all of us erst could ever do
by wile and wisdom. Lo, well can she say
whoso of women this warrior bore
among sons of men, if still she liveth,
that the God of the ages was good to her
in the birth of her bairn. Now, Beowulf, thee,
of heroes best, I shall heartily love
as mine own, my son; preserve thou ever
this kinship new: thou shalt never lack
wealth of the world that I wield as mine!
Full oft for less have I largess showered,
my precious hoard, on a punier man,
less stout in struggle. Thyself hast now
fulfilled such deeds, that thy fame shall endure
through all the ages. As ever he did,
well may the Wielder reward thee still!"
Beowulf spake, bairn of Ecgtheow: --
"This work of war most willingly
we have fought, this fight, and fearlessly dared

force of the foe. Fain, too, were I
hadst thou but seen himself, what time
the fiend in his trappings tottered to fall!
Swiftly, I thought, in strongest gripe
on his bed of death to bind him down,
that he in the hent of this hand of mine
should breathe his last: but he broke away.
Him I might not -- the Maker willed not --
hinder from flight, and firm enough hold
the life-destroyer: too sturdy was he,
the ruthless, in running! For rescue, however,
he left behind him his hand in pledge,
arm and shoulder; nor aught of help
could the cursed one thus procure at all.
None the longer liveth he, loathsome fiend,
sunk in his sins, but sorrow holds him
tightly grasped in gripe of anguish,
in baleful bonds, where bide he must,
evil outlaw, such awful doom
as the Mighty Maker shall mete him out."
More silent seemed the son of Ecglaf*
in boastful speech of his battle-deeds,
since athelings all, through the earl's great prowess,
beheld that hand, on the high roof gazing,
foeman's fingers, -- the forepart of each
of the sturdy nails to steel was likest, --
heathen's "hand-spear," hostile warrior's
claw uncanny. 'Twas clear, they said,
that him no blade of the brave could touch,
how keen soever, or cut away
that battle-hand bloody from baneful foe.

XV

THERE was hurry and hest in Heorot now
....
* Unferth, Beowulf's sometime opponent in the flyting.

for hands to bedeck it, and dense was the throng
of men and women the wine-hall to cleanse,
the guest-room to garnish. Gold-gay shone the hangings
that were wove on the wall, and wonders many
to delight each mortal that looks upon them.
Though braced within by iron bands,
that building bright was broken sorely;*
rent were its hinges; the roof alone
held safe and sound, when, seared with crime,
the fiendish foe his flight essayed,
of life despairing. -- No light thing that,
the flight for safety, -- essay it who will!
Forced of fate, he shall find his way
to the refuge ready for race of man,
for soul-possessors, and sons of earth;
and there his body on bed of death
shall rest after revel.
Arrived was the hour
when to hall proceeded Healfdene's son:
the king himself would sit to banquet.
Ne'er heard I of host in haughtier throng
more graciously gathered round giver-of-rings!
Bowed then to bench those bearers-of-glory,
fain of the feasting. Featly received
many a mead-cup the mighty-in-spirit,
kinsmen who sat in the sumptuous hall,
Hrothgar and Hrothulf. Heorot now
was filled with friends; the folk of Scyldings
ne'er yet had tried the traitor's deed.
To Beowulf gave the bairn of Healfdene
a gold-wove banner, guerdon of triumph,
broidered battle-flag, breastplate and helmet;
and a splendid sword was seen of many

* There is no horrible inconsistency here such as the critics strive
and cry about. In spite of the ruin that Grendel and Beowulf had
made within the hall, the framework and roof held firm, and swift
repairs made the interior habitable. Tapestries were hung on the
walls, and willing hands prepared the banquet.

borne to the brave one. Beowulf took
cup in hall: * for such costly gifts
he suffered no shame in that soldier throng.
For I heard of few heroes, in heartier mood,
with four such gifts, so fashioned with gold,
on the ale-bench honoring others thus!
O'er the roof of the helmet high, a ridge,
wound with wires, kept ward o'er the head,
lest the relict-of-files † should fierce invade,
sharp in the strife, when that shielded hero
should go to grapple against his foes.
Then the earls'-defence§ on the floor§ bade lead
coursers eight, with carven head-gear,
adown the hall: one horse was decked
with a saddle all shining and set in jewels;
'twas the battle-seat of the best of kings,
when to play of swords the son of Healfdene
was fain to fare. Ne'er failed his valor
in the crush of combat when corpses fell.
To Beowulf over them both then gave
the refuge-of-Ingwines right and power,
o'er war-steeds and weapons: wished him joy of them.
Manfully thus the mighty prince,
hoard-guard for heroes, that hard fight repaid
with steeds and treasures contemned by none
who is willing to say the sooth aright.

....

* From its formal use in other places, this phrase, to take cup in
hall, or "on the floor," would seem to mean that Beowulf stood
up to receive his gifts, drink to the donor, and say thanks.

† Kenning for sword.

‡ Hrothgar. He is also the "refuge of the friends of Ing," below.
Ing belongs to myth.

§ Horses are frequently led or ridden into the hall where folk sit
at banquet: so in Chaucer's Squire's tale, in the ballad of King
Estmere, and in the romances.

XVI

AND the lord of earls, to each that came
with Beowulf over the briny ways,
an heirloom there at the ale-bench gave,
precious gift; and the price[*] bade pay
in gold for him whom Grendel erst
murdered, -- and fain of them more had killed,
had not wisest God their Wyrd averted,
and the man's[†] brave mood. The Maker then
ruled human kind, as here and now.
Therefore is insight always best,
and forethought of mind. How much awaits him
of lief and of loath, who long time here,
through days of warfare this world endures!
Then song and music mingled sounds
in the presence of Healfdene's head-of-armies[‡]
and harping was heard with the hero-lay
as Hrothgar's singer the hall-joy woke
along the mead-seats, making his song
of that sudden raid on the sons of Finn.[§]
Healfdene's hero, Hnaef the Scylding,
was fated to fall in the Frisian slaughter.[¶]

....

* Man-price, wergild.

† Beowulf's.

‡ Hrothgar.

§ There is no need to assume a gap in the Ms. As before about
Sigemund and Heremod, so now, though at greater length, about
Finn and his feud, a lay is chanted or recited; and the epic poet,
counting on his readers' familiarity with the story, -- a fragment of
it still exists, -- simply gives the headings.

¶ The exact story to which this episode refers in summary is not
to be determined, but the following account of it is reasonable
and has good support among scholars. Finn, a Frisian chieftain,
who nevertheless has a "castle" outside the Frisian border,
marries Hildeburh, a Danish princess; and her brother, Hnaef,

Hildeburh needed not hold in value
her enemies' honor!* Innocent both
were the loved ones she lost at the linden-play,
bairn and brother, they bowed to fate,
stricken by spears; 'twas a sorrowful woman!
None doubted why the daughter of Hoc
bewailed her doom when dawning came,
and under the sky she saw them lying,
kinsmen murdered, where most she had kenned
of the sweets of the world! By war were swept, too,
Finn's own liegemen, and few were left;
in the parleying-place† he could ply no longer
weapon, nor war could he wage on Hengest,
and rescue his remnant by right of arms
from the prince's thane. A pact he offered:
another dwelling the Danes should have,
hall and high-seat, and half the power
should fall to them in Frisian land;
and at the fee-gifts, Folcwald's son
day by day the Danes should honor,
the folk of Hengest favor with rings,
even as truly, with treasure and jewels,
with fretted gold, as his Frisian kin
....

with many other Danes, pays Finn a visit. Relations between the
two peoples have been strained before. Something starts the old
feud anew; and the visitors are attacked in their quarters. Hnaef
is killed; so is a son of Hildeburh. Many fall on both sides. Peace
is patched up; a stately funeral is held; and the surviving visitors
become in a way vassals or liegemen of Finn, going back with
him to Frisia. So matters rest a while. Hengest is now leader of
the Danes; but he is set upon revenge for his former lord, Hnaef.
Probably he is killed in feud; but his clansmen, Guthlaf and Oslaf,
gather at their home a force of sturdy Danes, come back to Frisia,
storm Finn's stronghold, kill him, and carry back their kinswoman
Hildeburh.

* The "enemies" must be the Frisians.

† Battlefield. -- Hengest is the "prince's thane," companion of
Hnaef. "Folcwald's son" is Finn.

he meant to honor in ale-hall there.
Pact of peace they plighted further
on both sides firmly. Finn to Hengest
with oath, upon honor, openly promised
that woful remnant, with wise-men's aid,
nobly to govern, so none of the guests
by word or work should warp the treaty,[*]
or with malice of mind bemoan themselves
as forced to follow their fee-giver's slayer,
lordless men, as their lot ordained.
Should Frisian, moreover, with foeman's taunt,
that murderous hatred to mind recall,
then edge of the sword must seal his doom.
Oaths were given, and ancient gold
heaped from hoard. -- The hardy Scylding,
battle-thane best,[†] on his balefire lay.
All on the pyre were plain to see
the gory sark, the gilded swine-crest,
boar of hard iron, and athelings many
slain by the sword: at the slaughter they fell.
It was Hildeburh's hest, at Hnaef's own pyre
the bairn of her body on brands to lay,
his bones to burn, on the balefire placed,
at his uncle's side. In sorrowful dirges
bewept them the woman: great wailing ascended.
Then wound up to welkin the wildest of death-fires,
roared o'er the hillock:[‡] heads all were melted,
gashes burst, and blood gushed out
from bites[§] of the body. Balefire devoured,
....

* That is, Finn would govern in all honor the few Danish warriors
who were left, provided, of course, that none of them tried to
renew the quarrel or avenge Hnaef their fallen lord. If, again, one
of Finn's Frisians began a quarrel, he should die by the sword.

† Hnaef.

‡ The high place chosen for the funeral: see description of
Beowulf's funeral-pile at the end of the poem.

§ Wounds.

greediest spirit, those spared not by war
out of either folk: their flower was gone.

XVII

THEN hastened those heroes their home to see,
friendless, to find the Frisian land,
houses and high burg. Hengest still
through the death-dyed winter dwelt with Finn,
holding pact, yet of home he minded,
though powerless his ring-decked prow to drive
over the waters, now waves rolled fierce
lashed by the winds, or winter locked them
in icy fetters. Then fared another
year to men's dwellings, as yet they do,
the sunbright skies, that their season ever
duly await. Far off winter was driven;
fair lay earth's breast; and fain was the rover,
the guest, to depart, though more gladly he pondered
on wreaking his vengeance than roaming the deep,
and how to hasten the hot encounter
where sons of the Frisians were sure to be.
So he escaped not the common doom,
when Hun with "Lafing," the light-of-battle,
best of blades, his bosom pierced:
its edge was famed with the Frisian earls.
On fierce-heart Finn there fell likewise,
on himself at home, the horrid sword-death;
for Guthlaf and Oslaf of grim attack
had sorrowing told, from sea-ways landed,
mourning their woes.* Finn's wavering spirit
bode not in breast. The burg was reddened
with blood of foemen, and Finn was slain,

* That is, these two Danes, escaping home, had told the story of
the attack on Hnaef, the slaying of Hengest, and all the Danish
woes. Collecting a force, they return to Frisia and kill Finn in his
home.

king amid clansmen; the queen was taken.
To their ship the Scylding warriors bore
all the chattels the chieftain owned,
whatever they found in Finn's domain
of gems and jewels. The gentle wife
o'er paths of the deep to the Danes they bore,
led to her land.
The lay was finished,
the gleeman's song. Then glad rose the revel;
bench-joy brightened. Bearers draw
from their "wonder-vats" wine. Comes Wealhtheow forth,
under gold-crown goes where the good pair sit,
uncle and nephew, true each to the other one,
kindred in amity. Unferth the spokesman
at the Scylding lord's feet sat: men had faith in his spirit,
his keenness of courage, though kinsmen had found him
unsure at the sword-play. The Scylding queen spoke:
"Quaff of this cup, my king and lord,
breaker of rings, and blithe be thou,
gold-friend of men; to the Geats here speak
such words of mildness as man should use.
Be glad with thy Geats; of those gifts be mindful,
or near or far, which now thou hast.
Men say to me, as son thou wishest
yon hero to hold. Thy Heorot purged,
jewel-hall brightest, enjoy while thou canst,
with many a largess; and leave to thy kin
folk and realm when forth thou goest
to greet thy doom. For gracious I deem
my Hrothulf,* willing to hold and rule
....
* Nephew to Hrothgar, with whom he subsequently quarrels, and
elder cousin to the two young sons of Hrothgar and Wealhtheow,
-- their natural guardian in the event of the king's death. There is
something finely feminine in this speech of Wealhtheow's, apart
from its somewhat irregular and irrelevant sequence of topics.
Both she and her lord probably distrust Hrothulf; but she bids
the king to be of good cheer, and, turning to the suspect, heaps
affectionate assurances on his probity. "My own Hrothulf" will

nobly our youths, if thou yield up first,
prince of Scyldings, thy part in the world.
I ween with good he will well requite
offspring of ours, when all he minds
that for him we did in his helpless days
of gift and grace to gain him honor!"
Then she turned to the seat where her sons wereplaced,
Hrethric and Hrothmund, with heroes' bairns,
young men together: the Geat, too, sat there,
Beowulf brave, the brothers between.

XVIII

A CUP she gave him, with kindly greeting
and winsome words. Of wounden gold,
she offered, to honor him, arm-jewels twain,
corselet and rings, and of collars the noblest
that ever I knew the earth around.
Ne'er heard I so mighty, 'neath heaven's dome,
a hoard-gem of heroes, since Hama bore
to his bright-built burg the Brisings' necklace,
jewel and gem casket. -- Jealousy fled he,
Eormenric's hate: chose help eternal.
Hygelac Geat, grandson of Swerting,
on the last of his raids this ring bore with him,
under his banner the booty defending,
the war-spoil warding; but Wyrd o'erwhelmed him
what time, in his daring, dangers he sought,
feud with Frisians. Fairest of gems
he bore with him over the beaker-of-waves,
sovran strong: under shield he died.
Fell the corpse of the king into keeping of Franks,
gear of the breast, and that gorgeous ring;
weaker warriors won the spoil,

....
surely not forget these favors and benefits of the past, but will
repay them to the orphaned boy.

after gripe of battle, from Geatland's lord,
and held the death-field.
Din rose in hall.
Wealhtheow spake amid warriors, and said: --
"This jewel enjoy in thy jocund youth,
Beowulf lov'd, these battle-weeds wear,
a royal treasure, and richly thrive!
Preserve thy strength, and these striplings here
counsel in kindness: requital be mine.
Hast done such deeds, that for days to come
thou art famed among folk both far and near,
so wide as washeth the wave of Ocean
his windy walls. Through the ways of life
prosper, O prince! I pray for thee
rich possessions. To son of mine
be helpful in deed and uphold his joys!
Here every earl to the other is true,
mild of mood, to the master loyal!
Thanes are friendly, the throng obedient,
liegemen are revelling: list and obey!"
Went then to her place. -- That was proudest of feasts;
flowed wine for the warriors. Wyrd they knew not,
destiny dire, and the doom to be seen
by many an earl when eve should come,
and Hrothgar homeward hasten away,
royal, to rest. The room was guarded
by an army of earls, as erst was done.
They bared the bench-boards; abroad they spread
beds and bolsters. -- One beer-carouser
in danger of doom lay down in the hall. --
At their heads they set their shields of war,
bucklers bright; on the bench were there
over each atheling, easy to see,
the high battle-helmet, the haughty spear,
the corselet of rings. 'Twas their custom so
ever to be for battle prepared,
at home, or harrying, which it were,

even as oft as evil threatened
their sovran king. -- They were clansmen good.

XIX

THEN sank they to sleep. With sorrow one bought
his rest of the evening, -- as ofttime had happened
when Grendel guarded that golden hall,
evil wrought, till his end drew nigh,
slaughter for sins. 'Twas seen and told
how an avenger survived the fiend,
as was learned afar. The livelong time
after that grim fight, Grendel's mother,
monster of women, mourned her woe.
She was doomed to dwell in the dreary waters,
cold sea-courses, since Cain cut down
with edge of the sword his only brother,
his father's offspring: outlawed he fled,
marked with murder, from men's delights
warded the wilds. -- There woke from him
such fate-sent ghosts as Grendel, who,
war-wolf horrid, at Heorot found
a warrior watching and waiting the fray,
with whom the grisly one grappled amain.
But the man remembered his mighty power,
the glorious gift that God had sent him,
in his Maker's mercy put his trust
for comfort and help: so he conquered the foe,
felled the fiend, who fled abject,
reft of joy, to the realms of death,
mankind's foe. And his mother now,
gloomy and grim, would go that quest
of sorrow, the death of her son to avenge.
To Heorot came she, where helmeted Danes
slept in the hall. Too soon came back
old ills of the earls, when in she burst,

the mother of Grendel. Less grim, though, that terror,
e'en as terror of woman in war is less,
might of maid, than of men in arms
when, hammer-forged, the falchion hard,
sword gore-stained, through swine of the helm,
crested, with keen blade carves amain.
Then was in hall the hard-edge drawn,
the swords on the settles,* and shields a-many
firm held in hand: nor helmet minded
nor harness of mail, whom that horror seized.
Haste was hers; she would hie afar
and save her life when the liegemen saw her.
Yet a single atheling up she seized
fast and firm, as she fled to the moor.
He was for Hrothgar of heroes the dearest,
of trusty vassals betwixt the seas,
whom she killed on his couch, a clansman famous,
in battle brave. -- Nor was Beowulf there;
another house had been held apart,
after giving of gold, for the Geat renowned. --
Uproar filled Heorot; the hand all had viewed,
blood-flecked, she bore with her; bale was returned,
dole in the dwellings: 'twas dire exchange
where Dane and Geat were doomed to give
the lives of loved ones. Long-tried king,
the hoary hero, at heart was sad
when he knew his noble no more lived,
and dead indeed was his dearest thane.
To his bower was Beowulf brought in haste,
dauntless victor. As daylight broke,
along with his earls the atheling lord,
with his clansmen, came where the king abode
waiting to see if the Wielder-of-All
would turn this tale of trouble and woe.
Strode o'er floor the famed-in-strife,
with his hand-companions, -- the hall resounded, --
....
* They had laid their arms on the benches near where they slept.

wishing to greet the wise old king,
Ingwines' lord; he asked if the night
had passed in peace to the prince's mind.

XX

HROTHGAR spake, helmet-of-Scyldings: --
"Ask not of pleasure! Pain is renewed
to Danish folk. Dead is Aeschere,
of Yrmenlaf the elder brother,
my sage adviser and stay in council,
shoulder-comrade in stress of fight
when warriors clashed and we warded our heads,
hewed the helm-boars; hero famed
should be every earl as Aeschere was!
But here in Heorot a hand hath slain him
of wandering death-sprite. I wot not whither,*
proud of the prey, her path she took,
fain of her fill. The feud she avenged
that yesternight, unyieldingly,
Grendel in grimmest grasp thou killedst, --
seeing how long these liegemen mine
he ruined and ravaged. Reft of life,
in arms he fell. Now another comes,
keen and cruel, her kin to avenge,
faring far in feud of blood:
so that many a thane shall think, who e'er
sorrows in soul for that sharer of rings,
this is hardest of heart-bales. The hand lies low
that once was willing each wish to please.
Land-dwellers here† and liegemen mine,

....

* He surmises presently where she is.

† The connection is not difficult. The words of mourning, of
acute grief, are said; and according to Germanic sequence of
thought, inexorable here, the next and only topic is revenge.
But is it possible? Hrothgar leads up to his appeal and promise

who house by those parts, I have heard relate
that such a pair they have sometimes seen,
march-stalkers mighty the moorland haunting,
wandering spirits: one of them seemed,
so far as my folk could fairly judge,
of womankind; and one, accursed,
in man's guise trod the misery-track
of exile, though huger than human bulk.
Grendel in days long gone they named him,
folk of the land; his father they knew not,
nor any brood that was born to him
of treacherous spirits. Untrod is their home;
by wolf-cliffs haunt they and windy headlands,
fenways fearful, where flows the stream
from mountains gliding to gloom of the rocks,
underground flood. Not far is it hence
in measure of miles that the mere expands,
and o'er it the frost-bound forest hanging,
sturdily rooted, shadows the wave.
By night is a wonder weird to see,
fire on the waters. So wise lived none
of the sons of men, to search those depths!
Nay, though the heath-rover, harried by dogs,
the horn-proud hart, this holt should seek,
long distance driven, his dear life first
on the brink he yields ere he brave the plunge
to hide his head: 'tis no happy place!
Thence the welter of waters washes up
wan to welkin when winds bestir
evil storms, and air grows dusk,
and the heavens weep. Now is help once more
with thee alone! The land thou knowst not,
place of fear, where thou findest out
that sin-flecked being. Seek if thou dare!

....

with a skillful and often effective description of the horrors
which surround the monster's home and await the attempt of an
avenging foe.

I will reward thee, for waging this fight,
with ancient treasure, as erst I did,
with winding gold, if thou winnest back."

XXI

BEOWULF spake, bairn of Ecgtheow:
"Sorrow not, sage! It beseems us better
friends to avenge than fruitlessly mourn them.
Each of us all must his end abide
in the ways of the world; so win who may
glory ere death! When his days are told,
that is the warrior's worthiest doom.
Rise, O realm-warder! Ride we anon,
and mark the trail of the mother of Grendel.
No harbor shall hide her -- heed my promise! --
enfolding of field or forested mountain
or floor of the flood, let her flee where she will!
But thou this day endure in patience,
as I ween thou wilt, thy woes each one."
Leaped up the graybeard: God he thanked,
mighty Lord, for the man's brave words.
For Hrothgar soon a horse was saddled
wave-maned steed. The sovran wise
stately rode on; his shield-armed men
followed in force. The footprints led
along the woodland, widely seen,
a path o'er the plain, where she passed, and trod
the murky moor; of men-at-arms
she bore the bravest and best one, dead,
him who with Hrothgar the homestead ruled.
On then went the atheling-born
o'er stone-cliffs steep and strait defiles,
narrow passes and unknown ways,
headlands sheer, and the haunts of the Nicors.

Foremost he* fared, a few at his side
of the wiser men, the ways to scan,
till he found in a flash the forested hill
hanging over the hoary rock,
a woful wood: the waves below
were dyed in blood. The Danish men
had sorrow of soul, and for Scyldings all,
for many a hero, 'twas hard to bear,
ill for earls, when Aeschere's head
they found by the flood on the foreland there.
Waves were welling, the warriors saw,
hot with blood; but the horn sang oft
battle-song bold. The band sat down,
and watched on the water worm-like things,
sea-dragons strange that sounded the deep,
and nicors that lay on the ledge of the ness --
such as oft essay at hour of morn
on the road-of-sails their ruthless quest, --
and sea-snakes and monsters. These started away,
swollen and savage that song to hear,
that war-horn's blast. The warden of Geats,
with bolt from bow, then balked of life,
of wave-work, one monster, amid its heart
went the keen war-shaft; in water it seemed
less doughty in swimming whom death had seized.
Swift on the billows, with boar-spears well
hooked and barbed, it was hard beset,
done to death and dragged on the headland,
wave-roamer wondrous. Warriors viewed
the grisly guest.
Then girt him Beowulf
in martial mail, nor mourned for his life.
His breastplate broad and bright of hues,
woven by hand, should the waters try;
well could it ward the warrior's body
that battle should break on his breast in vain

....
* Hrothgar is probably meant.

nor harm his heart by the hand of a foe.
And the helmet white that his head protected
was destined to dare the deeps of the flood,
through wave-whirl win: 'twas wound with chains,
decked with gold, as in days of yore
the weapon-smith worked it wondrously,
with swine-forms set it, that swords nowise,
brandished in battle, could bite that helm.
Nor was that the meanest of mighty helps
which Hrothgar's orator offered at need:
"Hrunting" they named the hilted sword,
of old-time heirlooms easily first;
iron was its edge, all etched with poison,
with battle-blood hardened, nor blenched it at fight
in hero's hand who held it ever,
on paths of peril prepared to go
to folkstead* of foes. Not first time this
it was destined to do a daring task.
For he bore not in mind, the bairn of Ecglaf
sturdy and strong, that speech he had made,
drunk with wine, now this weapon he lent
to a stouter swordsman. Himself, though, durst not
under welter of waters wager his life
as loyal liegeman. So lost he his glory,
honor of earls. With the other not so,
who girded him now for the grim encounter.

XXII

BEOWULF spake, bairn of Ecgtheow: --
"Have mind, thou honored offspring of Healfdene
gold-friend of men, now I go on this quest,
sovran wise, what once was said:
if in thy cause it came that I
should lose my life, thou wouldst loyal bide

....
* Meeting place.

to me, though fallen, in father's place!
Be guardian, thou, to this group of my thanes,
my warrior-friends, if War should seize me;
and the goodly gifts thou gavest me,
Hrothgar beloved, to Hygelac send!
Geatland's king may ken by the gold,
Hrethel's son see, when he stares at the treasure,
that I got me a friend for goodness famed,
and joyed while I could in my jewel-bestower.
And let Unferth wield this wondrous sword,
earl far-honored, this heirloom precious,
hard of edge: with Hrunting I
seek doom of glory, or Death shall take me."
After these words the Weder-Geat lord
boldly hastened, biding never
answer at all: the ocean floods
closed o'er the hero. Long while of the day
fled ere he felt the floor of the sea.
Soon found the fiend who the flood-domain
sword-hungry held these hundred winters,
greedy and grim, that some guest from above,
some man, was raiding her monster-realm.
She grasped out for him with grisly claws,
and the warrior seized; yet scathed she not
his body hale; the breastplate hindered,
as she strove to shatter the sark of war,
the linked harness, with loathsome hand.
Then bore this brine-wolf, when bottom she touched,
the lord of rings to the lair she haunted
whiles vainly he strove, though his valor held,
weapon to wield against wondrous monsters
that sore beset him; sea-beasts many
tried with fierce tusks to tear his mail,
and swarmed on the stranger. But soon he marked
he was now in some hall, he knew not which,
where water never could work him harm,
nor through the roof could reach him ever

fangs of the flood. Firelight he saw,
beams of a blaze that brightly shone.
Then the warrior was ware of that wolf-of-the-deep,
mere-wife monstrous. For mighty stroke
he swung his blade, and the blow withheld not.
Then sang on her head that seemly blade
its war-song wild. But the warrior found
the light-of-battle* was loath to bite,
to harm the heart: its hard edge failed
the noble at need, yet had known of old
strife hand to hand, and had helmets cloven,
doomed men's fighting-gear. First time, this,
for the gleaming blade that its glory fell.
Firm still stood, nor failed in valor,
heedful of high deeds, Hygelac's kinsman;
flung away fretted sword, featly jewelled,
the angry earl; on earth it lay
steel-edged and stiff. His strength he trusted,
hand-gripe of might. So man shall do
whenever in war he weens to earn him
lasting fame, nor fears for his life!
Seized then by shoulder, shrank not from combat,
the Geatish war-prince Grendel's mother.
Flung then the fierce one, filled with wrath,
his deadly foe, that she fell to ground.
Swift on her part she paid him back
with grisly grasp, and grappled with him.
Spent with struggle, stumbled the warrior,
fiercest of fighting-men, fell adown.
On the hall-guest she hurled herself, hent her short sword,
broad and brown-edged,† the bairn to avenge,
the sole-born son. -- On his shoulder lay
braided breast-mail, barring death,

....

* Kenning for "sword." Hrunting is bewitched, laid under a spell
of uselessness, along with all other swords.

† This brown of swords, evidently meaning burnished, bright,
continues to be a favorite adjective in the popular ballads.

withstanding entrance of edge or blade.
Life would have ended for Ecgtheow's son,
under wide earth for that earl of Geats,
had his armor of war not aided him,
battle-net hard, and holy God
wielded the victory, wisest Maker.
The Lord of Heaven allowed his cause;
and easily rose the earl erect.

XXIII

'MID the battle-gear saw he a blade triumphant,
old-sword of Eotens, with edge of proof,
warriors' heirloom, weapon unmatched,
-- save only 'twas more than other men
to bandy-of-battle could bear at all --
as the giants had wrought it, ready and keen.
Seized then its chain-hilt the Scyldings' chieftain,
bold and battle-grim, brandished the sword,
reckless of life, and so wrathfully smote
that it gripped her neck and grasped her hard,
her bone-rings breaking: the blade pierced through
that fated-one's flesh: to floor she sank.
Bloody the blade: he was blithe of his deed.
Then blazed forth light. 'Twas bright within
as when from the sky there shines unclouded
heaven's candle. The hall he scanned.
By the wall then went he; his weapon raised
high by its hilts the Hygelac-thane,
angry and eager. That edge was not useless
to the warrior now. He wished with speed
Grendel to guerdon for grim raids many,
for the war he waged on Western-Danes
oftener far than an only time,
when of Hrothgar's hearth-companions
he slew in slumber, in sleep devoured,

fifteen men of the folk of Danes,
and as many others outward bore,
his horrible prey. Well paid for that
the wrathful prince! For now prone he saw
Grendel stretched there, spent with war,
spoiled of life, so scathed had left him
Heorot's battle. The body sprang far
when after death it endured the blow,
sword-stroke savage, that severed its head.
Soon,* then, saw the sage companions
who waited with Hrothgar, watching the flood,
that the tossing waters turbid grew,
blood-stained the mere. Old men together,
hoary-haired, of the hero spake;
the warrior would not, they weened, again,
proud of conquest, come to seek
their mighty master. To many it seemed
the wolf-of-the-waves had won his life.
The ninth hour came. The noble Scyldings
left the headland; homeward went
the gold-friend of men.† But the guests sat on,
stared at the surges, sick in heart,
and wished, yet weened not, their winsome lord
again to see.
Now that sword began,
from blood of the fight, in battle-droppings,‡
war-blade, to wane: 'twas a wondrous thing
that all of it melted as ice is wont
when frosty fetters the Father loosens,
unwinds the wave-bonds, wielding all
seasons and times: the true God he!
Nor took from that dwelling the duke of the Geats
save only the head and that hilt withal
blazoned with jewels: the blade had melted,
....

* After the killing of the monster and Grendel's decapitation.

† Hrothgar.

‡ The blade slowly dissolves in blood-stained drops like icicles.

burned was the bright sword, her blood was so hot,
so poisoned the hell-sprite who perished within there.
Soon he was swimming who safe saw in combat
downfall of demons; up-dove through the flood.
The clashing waters were cleansed now,
waste of waves, where the wandering fiend
her life-days left and this lapsing world.
Swam then to strand the sailors'-refuge,
sturdy-in-spirit, of sea-booty glad,
of burden brave he bore with him.
Went then to greet him, and God they thanked,
the thane-band choice of their chieftain blithe,
that safe and sound they could see him again.
Soon from the hardy one helmet and armor
deftly they doffed: now drowsed the mere,
water 'neath welkin, with war-blood stained.
Forth they fared by the footpaths thence,
merry at heart the highways measured,
well-known roads. Courageous men
carried the head from the cliff by the sea,
an arduous task for all the band,
the firm in fight, since four were needed
on the shaft-of-slaughter* strenuously
to bear to the gold-hall Grendel's head.
So presently to the palace there
foemen fearless, fourteen Geats,
marching came. Their master-of-clan
mighty amid them the meadow-ways trod.
Strode then within the sovran thane
fearless in fight, of fame renowned,
hardy hero, Hrothgar to greet.
And next by the hair into hall was borne
Grendel's head, where the henchmen were drinking,
an awe to clan and queen alike,
a monster of marvel: the men looked on.

....
* Spear.

XXIV

BEOWULF spake, bairn of Ecgtheow: --
"Lo, now, this sea-booty, son of Healfdene,
Lord of Scyldings, we've lustily brought thee,
sign of glory; thou seest it here.
Not lightly did I with my life escape!
In war under water this work I essayed
with endless effort; and even so
my strength had been lost had the Lord not shielded me.
Not a whit could I with Hrunting do
in work of war, though the weapon is good;
yet a sword the Sovran of Men vouchsafed me
to spy on the wall there, in splendor hanging,
old, gigantic, -- how oft He guides
the friendless wight! -- and I fought with that brand,
felling in fight, since fate was with me,
the house's wardens. That war-sword then
all burned, bright blade, when the blood gushed o'er it,
battle-sweat hot; but the hilt I brought back
from my foes. So avenged I their fiendish deeds
death-fall of Danes, as was due and right.
And this is my hest, that in Heorot now
safe thou canst sleep with thy soldier band,
and every thane of all thy folk
both old and young; no evil fear,
Scyldings' lord, from that side again,
aught ill for thy earls, as erst thou must!"
Then the golden hilt, for that gray-haired leader,
hoary hero, in hand was laid,
giant-wrought, old. So owned and enjoyed it
after downfall of devils, the Danish lord,
wonder-smiths' work, since the world was rid
of that grim-souled fiend, the foe of God,
murder-marked, and his mother as well.
Now it passed into power of the people's king,

best of all that the oceans bound
who have scattered their gold o'er Scandia's isle.
Hrothgar spake -- the hilt he viewed,
heirloom old, where was etched the rise
of that far-off fight when the floods o'erwhelmed,
raging waves, the race of giants
(fearful their fate!), a folk estranged
from God Eternal: whence guerdon due
in that waste of waters the Wielder paid them.
So on the guard of shining gold
in runic staves it was rightly said
for whom the serpent-traced sword was wrought,
best of blades, in bygone days,
and the hilt well wound. -- The wise-one spake,
son of Healfdene; silent were all: --
"Lo, so may he say who sooth and right
follows 'mid folk, of far times mindful,
a land-warden old,* that this earl belongs
to the better breed! So, borne aloft,
thy fame must fly, O friend my Beowulf,
far and wide o'er folksteads many. Firmly thou
shalt all maintain,
mighty strength with mood of wisdom. Love of
mine will I assure thee,
as, awhile ago, I promised; thou shalt prove a stay
in future,
in far-off years, to folk of thine,
to the heroes a help. Was not Heremod thus
to offspring of Ecgwela, Honor-Scyldings,
nor grew for their grace, but for grisly slaughter,
for doom of death to the Danishmen.
He slew, wrath-swollen, his shoulder-comrades,
companions at board! So he passed alone,
chieftain haughty, from human cheer.

....
* That is, "whoever has as wide authority as I have and can
remember so far back so many instances of heroism, may well
say, as I say, that no better hero ever lived than Beowulf."

Though him the Maker with might endowed,
delights of power, and uplifted high
above all men, yet blood-fierce his mind,
his breast-hoard, grew, no bracelets gave he
to Danes as was due; he endured all joyless
strain of struggle and stress of woe,
long feud with his folk. Here find thy lesson!
Of virtue advise thee! This verse I have said for thee,
wise from lapsed winters. Wondrous seems
how to sons of men Almighty God
in the strength of His spirit sendeth wisdom,
estate, high station: He swayeth all things.
Whiles He letteth right lustily fare
the heart of the hero of high-born race, --
in seat ancestral assigns him bliss,
his folk's sure fortress in fee to hold,
puts in his power great parts of the earth,
empire so ample, that end of it
this wanter-of-wisdom weeneth none.
So he waxes in wealth, nowise can harm him
illness or age; no evil cares
shadow his spirit; no sword-hate threatens
from ever an enemy: all the world
wends at his will, no worse he knoweth,
till all within him obstinate pride
waxes and wakes while the warden slumbers,
the spirit's sentry; sleep is too fast
which masters his might, and the murderer nears,
stealthily shooting the shafts from his bow!

XXV

"UNDER harness his heart then is hit indeed
by sharpest shafts; and no shelter avails
from foul behest of the hellish fiend.*
....
* That is, he is now undefended by conscience from the

Him seems too little what long he possessed.
Greedy and grim, no golden rings
he gives for his pride; the promised future
forgets he and spurns, with all God has sent him,
Wonder-Wielder, of wealth and fame.
Yet in the end it ever comes
that the frame of the body fragile yields,
fated falls; and there follows another
who joyously the jewels divides,
the royal riches, nor recks of his forebear.
Ban, then, such baleful thoughts, Beowulf dearest,
best of men, and the better part choose,
profit eternal; and temper thy pride,
warrior famous! The flower of thy might
lasts now a while: but erelong it shall be
that sickness or sword thy strength shall minish,
or fang of fire, or flooding billow,
or bite of blade, or brandished spear,
or odious age; or the eyes' clear beam
wax dull and darken: Death even thee
in haste shall o'erwhelm, thou hero of war!
So the Ring-Danes these half-years a hundred I ruled,
wielded 'neath welkin, and warded them bravely
from mighty-ones many o'er middle-earth,
from spear and sword, till it seemed for me
no foe could be found under fold of the sky.
Lo, sudden the shift! To me seated secure
came grief for joy when Grendel began
to harry my home, the hellish foe;
for those ruthless raids, unresting I suffered
heart-sorrow heavy. Heaven be thanked,
Lord Eternal, for life extended
that I on this head all hewn and bloody,
after long evil, with eyes may gaze!
-- Go to the bench now! Be glad at banquet,
warrior worthy! A wealth of treasure
....
temptations (shafts) of the devil.

at dawn of day, be dealt between us!"
Glad was the Geats' lord, going betimes
to seek his seat, as the Sage commanded.
Afresh, as before, for the famed-in-battle,
for the band of the hall, was a banquet dight
nobly anew. The Night-Helm darkened
dusk o'er the drinkers.
The doughty ones rose:
for the hoary-headed would hasten to rest,
aged Scylding; and eager the Geat,
shield-fighter sturdy, for sleeping yearned.
Him wander-weary, warrior-guest
from far, a hall-thane heralded forth,
who by custom courtly cared for all
needs of a thane as in those old days
warrior-wanderers wont to have.
So slumbered the stout-heart. Stately the hall
rose gabled and gilt where the guest slept on
till a raven black the rapture-of-heaven*
blithe-heart boded. Bright came flying
shine after shadow. The swordsmen hastened,
athelings all were eager homeward
forth to fare; and far from thence
the great-hearted guest would guide his keel.
Bade then the hardy-one Hrunting be brought
to the son of Ecglaf, the sword bade him take,
excellent iron, and uttered his thanks for it,
quoth that he counted it keen in battle,
"war-friend" winsome: with words he slandered not
edge of the blade: 'twas a big-hearted man!
Now eager for parting and armed at point
warriors waited, while went to his host
that Darling of Danes. The doughty atheling
to high-seat hastened and Hrothgar greeted.

....

* Kenning for the sun. -- This is a strange role for the raven. He is
the warrior's bird of battle, exults in slaughter and carnage; his joy
here is a compliment to the sunrise.

XXVI

BEOWULF spake, bairn of Ecgtheow: --
"Lo, we seafarers say our will,
far-come men, that we fain would seek
Hygelac now. We here have found
hosts to our heart: thou hast harbored us well.
If ever on earth I am able to win me
more of thy love, O lord of men,
aught anew, than I now have done,
for work of war I am willing still!
If it come to me ever across the seas
that neighbor foemen annoy and fright thee, --
as they that hate thee erewhile have used, --
thousands then of thanes I shall bring,
heroes to help thee. Of Hygelac I know,
ward of his folk, that, though few his years,
the lord of the Geats will give me aid
by word and by work, that well I may serve thee,
wielding the war-wood to win thy triumph
and lending thee might when thou lackest men.
If thy Hrethric should come to court of Geats,
a sovran's son, he will surely there
find his friends. A far-off land
each man should visit who vaunts him brave."
Him then answering, Hrothgar spake: --
"These words of thine the wisest God
sent to thy soul! No sager counsel
from so young in years e'er yet have I heard.
Thou art strong of main and in mind art wary,
art wise in words! I ween indeed
if ever it hap that Hrethel's heir
by spear be seized, by sword-grim battle,
by illness or iron, thine elder and lord,
people's leader, -- and life be thine, --
no seemlier man will the Sea-Geats find

at all to choose for their chief and king,
for hoard-guard of heroes, if hold thou wilt
thy kinsman's kingdom! Thy keen mind pleases me
the longer the better, Beowulf loved!
Thou hast brought it about that both our peoples,
sons of the Geat and Spear-Dane folk,
shall have mutual peace, and from murderous strife,
such as once they waged, from war refrain.
Long as I rule this realm so wide,
let our hoards be common, let heroes with gold
each other greet o'er the gannet's-bath,
and the ringed-prow bear o'er rolling waves
tokens of love. I trow my landfolk
towards friend and foe are firmly joined,
and honor they keep in the olden way."
To him in the hall, then, Healfdene's son
gave treasures twelve, and the trust-of-earls
bade him fare with the gifts to his folk beloved,
hale to his home, and in haste return.
Then kissed the king of kin renowned,
Scyldings' chieftain, that choicest thane,
and fell on his neck. Fast flowed the tears
of the hoary-headed. Heavy with winters,
he had chances twain, but he clung to this,* --
that each should look on the other again,
and hear him in hall. Was this hero so dear to him.
his breast's wild billows he banned in vain;
safe in his soul a secret longing,
locked in his mind, for that loved man
burned in his blood. Then Beowulf strode,
glad of his gold-gifts, the grass-plot o'er,
warrior blithe. The wave-roamer bode
riding at anchor, its owner awaiting.
As they hastened onward, Hrothgar's gift

* That is, he might or might not see Beowulf again. Old as he
was, the latter chance was likely; but he clung to the former,
hoping to see his young friend again "and exchange brave words
in the hall."

they lauded at length. -- 'Twas a lord unpeered,
every way blameless, till age had broken
-- it spareth no mortal -- his splendid might.

XXVII

CAME now to ocean the ever-courageous
hardy henchmen, their harness bearing,
woven war-sarks. The warden marked,
trusty as ever, the earl's return.
From the height of the hill no hostile words
reached the guests as he rode to greet them;
but "Welcome!" he called to that Weder clan
as the sheen-mailed spoilers to ship marched on.
Then on the strand, with steeds and treasure
and armor their roomy and ring-dight ship
was heavily laden: high its mast
rose over Hrothgar's hoarded gems.
A sword to the boat-guard Beowulf gave,
mounted with gold; on the mead-bench since
he was better esteemed, that blade possessing,
heirloom old. -- Their ocean-keel boarding,
they drove through the deep, and Daneland left.
A sea-cloth was set, a sail with ropes,
firm to the mast; the flood-timbers moaned;*
nor did wind over billows that wave-swimmer blow
across from her course. The craft sped on,
foam-necked it floated forth o'er the waves,
keel firm-bound over briny currents,
till they got them sight of the Geatish cliffs,
home-known headlands. High the boat,
stirred by winds, on the strand updrove.
Helpful at haven the harbor-guard stood,
who long already for loved companions
by the water had waited and watched afar.
....
* With the speed of the boat.

He bound to the beach the broad-bosomed ship
with anchor-bands, lest ocean-billows
that trusty timber should tear away.
Then Beowulf bade them bear the treasure,
gold and jewels; no journey far
was it thence to go to the giver of rings,
Hygelac Hrethling: at home he dwelt
by the sea-wall close, himself and clan.
Haughty that house, a hero the king,
high the hall, and Hygd* right young,
wise and wary, though winters few
in those fortress walls she had found a home,
Haereth's daughter. Nor humble her ways,
nor grudged she gifts to the Geatish men,
of precious treasure. Not Thryth's pride showed she,
folk-queen famed, or that fell deceit.
Was none so daring that durst make bold
(save her lord alone) of the liegemen dear
that lady full in the face to look,
but forged fetters he found his lot,
bonds of death! And brief the respite;
soon as they seized him, his sword-doom was spoken,
and the burnished blade a baleful murder
proclaimed and closed. No queenly way
for woman to practise, though peerless she,
that the weaver-of-peace† from warrior dear
by wrath and lying his life should reave!
But Hemming's kinsman hindered this. --
For over their ale men also told
that of these folk-horrors fewer she wrought,
onslaughts of evil, after she went,
gold-decked bride, to the brave young prince,
atheling haughty, and Offa's hall
o'er the fallow flood at her father's bidding
....

* Queen to Hygelac. She is praised by contrast with the antitype,
Thryth, just as Beowulf was praised by contrast with Heremod.

† Kenning for "wife."

safely sought, where since she prospered,
royal, throned, rich in goods,
fain of the fair life fate had sent her,
and leal in love to the lord of warriors.
He, of all heroes I heard of ever
from sea to sea, of the sons of earth,
most excellent seemed. Hence Offa was praised
for his fighting and feeing by far-off men,
the spear-bold warrior; wisely he ruled
over his empire. Eomer woke to him,
help of heroes, Hemming's kinsman,
Grandson of Garmund, grim in war.

XXVIII

HASTENED the hardy one, henchmen with him,
sandy strand of the sea to tread
and widespread ways. The world's great candle,
sun shone from south. They strode along
with sturdy steps to the spot they knew
where the battle-king young, his burg within,
slayer of Ongentheow, shared the rings,
shelter-of-heroes. To Hygelac
Beowulf's coming was quickly told, --
that there in the court the clansmen's refuge,
the shield-companion sound and alive,
hale from the hero-play homeward strode.
With haste in the hall, by highest order,
room for the rovers was readily made.
By his sovran he sat, come safe from battle,
kinsman by kinsman. His kindly lord
he first had greeted in gracious form,
with manly words. The mead dispensing,
came through the high hall Haereth's daughter,
winsome to warriors, wine-cup bore
to the hands of the heroes. Hygelac then

his comrade fairly with question plied
in the lofty hall, sore longing to know
what manner of sojourn the Sea-Geats made.
"What came of thy quest, my kinsman Beowulf,
when thy yearnings suddenly swept thee yonder
battle to seek o'er the briny sea,
combat in Heorot? Hrothgar couldst thou
aid at all, the honored chief,
in his wide-known woes? With waves of care
my sad heart seethed; I sore mistrusted
my loved one's venture: long I begged thee
by no means to seek that slaughtering monster,
but suffer the South-Danes to settle their feud
themselves with Grendel. Now God be thanked
that safe and sound I can see thee now!"
Beowulf spake, the bairn of Ecgtheow: --
"'Tis known and unhidden, Hygelac Lord,
to many men, that meeting of ours,
struggle grim between Grendel and me,
which we fought on the field where full too many
sorrows he wrought for the Scylding-Victors,
evils unending. These all I avenged.
No boast can be from breed of Grendel,
any on earth, for that uproar at dawn,
from the longest-lived of the loathsome race
in fleshly fold! -- But first I went
Hrothgar to greet in the hall of gifts,
where Healfdene's kinsman high-renowned,
soon as my purpose was plain to him,
assigned me a seat by his son and heir.
The liegemen were lusty; my life-days never
such merry men over mead in hall
have I heard under heaven! The high-born queen,
people's peace-bringer, passed through the hall,
cheered the young clansmen, clasps of gold,
ere she sought her seat, to sundry gave.
Oft to the heroes Hrothgar's daughter,

to earls in turn, the ale-cup tendered, --
she whom I heard these hall-companions
Freawaru name, when fretted gold
she proffered the warriors. Promised is she,
gold-decked maid, to the glad son of Froda.
Sage this seems to the Scylding's-friend,
kingdom's-keeper: he counts it wise
the woman to wed so and ward off feud,
store of slaughter. But seldom ever
when men are slain, does the murder-spear sink
but briefest while, though the bride be fair!*
"Nor haply will like it the Heathobard lord,
and as little each of his liegemen all,
when a thane of the Danes, in that doughty throng,
goes with the lady along their hall,
and on him the old-time heirlooms glisten
hard and ring-decked, Heathobard's treasure,
weapons that once they wielded fair
until they lost at the linden-play†
liegeman leal and their lives as well.

* Beowulf gives his uncle the king not mere gossip of his journey,
but a statesmanlike forecast of the outcome of certain policies at
the Danish court. Talk of interpolation here is absurd. As both
Beowulf and Hygelac know, -- and the folk for whom the Beow-
ulf was put together also knew, -- Froda was king of the Heatho-
bards (probably the Langobards, once near neighbors of Angle
and Saxon tribes on the continent), and had fallen in fight with
the Danes. Hrothgar will set aside this feud by giving his daugh-
ter as "peace-weaver" and wife to the young king Ingeld, son of
the slain Froda. But Beowulf, on general principles and from his
observation of the particular case, foretells trouble.

† Play of shields, battle. A Danish warrior cuts down Froda in
the fight, and takes his sword and armor, leaving them to a son.
This son is selected to accompany his mistress, the young princess
Freawaru, to her new home when she is Ingeld's queen. Heed-
lessly he wears the sword of Froda in hall. An old warrior points
it out to Ingeld, and eggs him on to vengeance. At his instigation
the Dane is killed; but the murderer, afraid of results, and know-
ing the land, escapes. So the old feud must break out again.

Then, over the ale, on this heirloom gazing,
some ash-wielder old who has all in mind
that spear-death of men,* -- he is stern of mood,
heavy at heart, -- in the hero young
tests the temper and tries the soul
and war-hate wakens, with words like these: --
Canst thou not, comrade, ken that sword
which to the fray thy father carried
in his final feud, 'neath the fighting-mask,
dearest of blades, when the Danish slew him
and wielded the war-place on Withergild's fall,
after havoc of heroes, those hardy Scyldings?
Now, the son of a certain slaughtering Dane,
proud of his treasure, paces this hall,
joys in the killing, and carries the jewel†
that rightfully ought to be owned by thee!_
Thus he urges and eggs him all the time
with keenest words, till occasion offers
that Freawaru's thane, for his father's deed,
after bite of brand in his blood must slumber,
losing his life; but that liegeman flies
living away, for the land he kens.
And thus be broken on both their sides
oaths of the earls, when Ingeld's breast
wells with war-hate, and wife-love now
after the care-billows cooler grows.
"So‡ I hold not high the Heathobards' faith
due to the Danes, or their during love
and pact of peace. -- But I pass from that,
turning to Grendel, O giver-of-treasure,
and saying in full how the fight resulted,
hand-fray of heroes. When heaven's jewel
....

* That is, their disastrous battle and the slaying of their king.

† The sword.

‡ Beowulf returns to his forecast. Things might well go somewhat
as follows, he says; sketches a little tragic story; and with this
prophecy by illustration returns to the tale of his adventure.

had fled o'er far fields, that fierce sprite came,
night-foe savage, to seek us out
where safe and sound we sentried the hall.
To Hondscio then was that harassing deadly,
his fall there was fated. He first was slain,
girded warrior. Grendel on him
turned murderous mouth, on our mighty kinsman,
and all of the brave man's body devoured.
Yet none the earlier, empty-handed,
would the bloody-toothed murderer, mindful of bale,
outward go from the gold-decked hall:
but me he attacked in his terror of might,
with greedy hand grasped me. A glove hung by him*
wide and wondrous, wound with bands;
and in artful wise it all was wrought,
by devilish craft, of dragon-skins.
Me therein, an innocent man,
the fiendish foe was fain to thrust
with many another. He might not so,
when I all angrily upright stood.
'Twere long to relate how that land-destroyer
I paid in kind for his cruel deeds;
yet there, my prince, this people of thine
got fame by my fighting. He fled away,
and a little space his life preserved;
but there staid behind him his stronger hand
left in Heorot; heartsick thence
on the floor of the ocean that outcast fell.
Me for this struggle the Scyldings'-friend
paid in plenty with plates of gold,
with many a treasure, when morn had come
and we all at the banquet-board sat down.
Then was song and glee. The gray-haired Scylding,
much tested, told of the times of yore.
Whiles the hero his harp bestirred,
wood-of-delight; now lays he chanted
....
* Not an actual glove, but a sort of bag.

of sooth and sadness, or said aright
legends of wonder, the wide-hearted king;
or for years of his youth he would yearn at times,
for strength of old struggles, now stricken with age,
hoary hero: his heart surged full
when, wise with winters, he wailed their flight.
Thus in the hall the whole of that day
at ease we feasted, till fell o'er earth
another night. Anon full ready
in greed of vengeance, Grendel's mother
set forth all doleful. Dead was her son
through war-hate of Weders; now, woman monstrous
with fury fell a foeman she slew,
avenged her offspring. From Aeschere old,
loyal councillor, life was gone;
nor might they e'en, when morning broke,
those Danish people, their death-done comrade
burn with brands, on balefire lay
the man they mourned. Under mountain stream
she had carried the corpse with cruel hands.
For Hrothgar that was the heaviest sorrow
of all that had laden the lord of his folk.
The leader then, by thy life, besought me
(sad was his soul) in the sea-waves' coil
to play the hero and hazard my being
for glory of prowess: my guerdon he pledged.
I then in the waters -- 'tis widely known --
that sea-floor-guardian savage found.
Hand-to-hand there a while we struggled;
billows welled blood; in the briny hall
her head I hewed with a hardy blade
from Grendel's mother, -- and gained my life,
though not without danger. My doom was not yet.
Then the haven-of-heroes, Healfdene's son,
gave me in guerdon great gifts of price.

XXIX

"So held this king to the customs old,
that I wanted for nought in the wage I gained,
the meed of my might; he made me gifts,
Healfdene's heir, for my own disposal.
Now to thee, my prince, I proffer them all,
gladly give them. Thy grace alone
can find me favor. Few indeed
have I of kinsmen, save, Hygelac, thee!"
Then he bade them bear him the boar-head standard,
the battle-helm high, and breastplate gray,
the splendid sword; then spake in form: --
"Me this war-gear the wise old prince,
Hrothgar, gave, and his hest he added,
that its story be straightway said to thee. --
A while it was held by Heorogar king,
for long time lord of the land of Scyldings;
yet not to his son the sovran left it,
to daring Heoroweard, -- dear as he was to him,
his harness of battle. -- Well hold thou it all!"
And I heard that soon passed o'er the path of this treasure,
all apple-fallow, four good steeds,
each like the others, arms and horses
he gave to the king. So should kinsmen be,
not weave one another the net of wiles,
or with deep-hid treachery death contrive
for neighbor and comrade. His nephew was ever
by hardy Hygelac held full dear,
and each kept watch o'er the other's weal.
I heard, too, the necklace to Hygd he presented,
wonder-wrought treasure, which Wealhtheow gave him
sovran's daughter: three steeds he added,
slender and saddle-gay. Since such gift
the gem gleamed bright on the breast of the queen.
Thus showed his strain the son of Ecgtheow

as a man remarked for mighty deeds
and acts of honor. At ale he slew not
comrade or kin; nor cruel his mood,
though of sons of earth his strength was greatest,
a glorious gift that God had sent
the splendid leader. Long was he spurned,
and worthless by Geatish warriors held;
him at mead the master-of-clans
failed full oft to favor at all.
Slack and shiftless the strong men deemed him,
profitless prince; but payment came,
to the warrior honored, for all his woes. --
Then the bulwark-of-earls* bade bring within,
hardy chieftain, Hrethel's heirloom
garnished with gold: no Geat e'er knew
in shape of a sword a statelier prize.
The brand he laid in Beowulf's lap;
and of hides assigned him seven thousand,[†]
with house and high-seat. They held in common
land alike by their line of birth,
inheritance, home: but higher the king
because of his rule o'er the realm itself.
Now further it fell with the flight of years,
with harryings horrid, that Hygelac perished,[‡]
and Heardred, too, by hewing of swords
under the shield-wall slaughtered lay,
when him at the van of his victor-folk
sought hardy heroes, Heatho-Scilfings,
in arms o'erwhelming Hereric's nephew.
Then Beowulf came as king this broad

....

* Hygelac.

† This is generally assumed to mean hides, though the text simply
says "seven thousand." A hide in England meant about 120 acres,
though "the size of the acre varied."

‡ On the historical raid into Frankish territory between 512 and
520 A.D. The subsequent course of events, as gathered from
hints of this epic, is partly told in Scandinavian legend.

realm to wield; and he ruled it well
fifty winters,* a wise old prince,
warding his land, until One began
in the dark of night, a Dragon, to rage.
In the grave on the hill a hoard it guarded,
in the stone-barrow steep. A strait path reached it,
unknown to mortals. Some man, however,
came by chance that cave within
to the heathen hoard.† In hand he took
a golden goblet, nor gave he it back,
stole with it away, while the watcher slept,
by thievish wiles: for the warden's wrath
prince and people must pay betimes!

XXX

THAT way he went with no will of his own,
in danger of life, to the dragon's hoard,
but for pressure of peril, some prince's thane.
He fled in fear the fatal scourge,
seeking shelter, a sinful man,
and entered in. At the awful sight

....

* The chronology of this epic, as scholars have worked it out,
would make Beowulf well over ninety years of age when he fights
the dragon. But the fifty years of his reign need not be taken as
historical fact.

† The text is here hopelessly illegible, and only the general drift
of the meaning can be rescued. For one thing, we have the old
myth of a dragon who guards hidden treasure. But with this
runs the story of some noble, last of his race, who hides all his
wealth within this barrow and there chants his farewell to life's
glories. After his death the dragon takes possession of the hoard
and watches over it. A condemned or banished man, desperate,
hides in the barrow, discovers the treasure, and while the dragon
sleeps, makes off with a golden beaker or the like, and carries it
for propitiation to his master. The dragon discovers the loss and
exacts fearful penalty from the people round about.

tottered that guest, and terror seized him;
yet the wretched fugitive rallied anon
from fright and fear ere he fled away,
and took the cup from that treasure-hoard.
Of such besides there was store enough,
heirlooms old, the earth below,
which some earl forgotten, in ancient years,
left the last of his lofty race,
heedfully there had hidden away,
dearest treasure. For death of yore
had hurried all hence; and he alone
left to live, the last of the clan,
weeping his friends, yet wished to bide
warding the treasure, his one delight,
though brief his respite. The barrow, new-ready,
to strand and sea-waves stood anear,
hard by the headland, hidden and closed;
there laid within it his lordly heirlooms
and heaped hoard of heavy gold
that warden of rings. Few words he spake:
"Now hold thou, earth, since heroes may not,
what earls have owned! Lo, erst from thee
brave men brought it! But battle-death seized
and cruel killing my clansmen all,
robbed them of life and a liegeman's joys.
None have I left to lift the sword,
or to cleanse the carven cup of price,
beaker bright. My brave are gone.
And the helmet hard, all haughty with gold,
shall part from its plating. Polishers sleep
who could brighten and burnish the battle-mask;
and those weeds of war that were wont to brave
over bicker of shields the bite of steel
rust with their bearer. The ringed mail
fares not far with famous chieftain,
at side of hero! No harp's delight,
no glee-wood's gladness! No good hawk now

flies through the hall! Nor horses fleet
stamp in the burgstead! Battle and death
the flower of my race have reft away."
Mournful of mood, thus he moaned his woe,
alone, for them all, and unblithe wept
by day and by night, till death's fell wave
o'erwhelmed his heart. His hoard-of-bliss
that old ill-doer open found,
who, blazing at twilight the barrows haunteth,
naked foe-dragon flying by night
folded in fire: the folk of earth
dread him sore. 'Tis his doom to seek
hoard in the graves, and heathen gold
to watch, many-wintered: nor wins he thereby!
Powerful this plague-of-the-people thus
held the house of the hoard in earth
three hundred winters; till One aroused
wrath in his breast, to the ruler bearing
that costly cup, and the king implored
for bond of peace. So the barrow was plundered,
borne off was booty. His boon was granted
that wretched man; and his ruler saw
first time what was fashioned in far-off days.
When the dragon awoke, new woe was kindled.
O'er the stone he snuffed. The stark-heart found
footprint of foe who so far had gone
in his hidden craft by the creature's head. --
So may the undoomed easily flee
evils and exile, if only he gain
the grace of The Wielder! -- That warden of gold
o'er the ground went seeking, greedy to find
the man who wrought him such wrong in sleep.
Savage and burning, the barrow he circled
all without; nor was any there,
none in the waste.... Yet war he desired,
was eager for battle. The barrow he entered,
sought the cup, and discovered soon

that some one of mortals had searched his treasure,
his lordly gold. The guardian waited
ill-enduring till evening came;
boiling with wrath was the barrow's keeper,
and fain with flame the foe to pay
for the dear cup's loss. -- Now day was fled
as the worm had wished. By its wall no more
was it glad to bide, but burning flew
folded in flame: a fearful beginning
for sons of the soil; and soon it came,
in the doom of their lord, to a dreadful end.

XXXI

THEN the baleful fiend its fire belched out,
and bright homes burned. The blaze stood high
all landsfolk frighting. No living thing
would that loathly one leave as aloft it flew.
Wide was the dragon's warring seen,
its fiendish fury far and near,
as the grim destroyer those Geatish people
hated and hounded. To hidden lair,
to its hoard it hastened at hint of dawn.
Folk of the land it had lapped in flame,
with bale and brand. In its barrow it trusted,
its battling and bulwarks: that boast was vain!
To Beowulf then the bale was told
quickly and truly: the king's own home,
of buildings the best, in brand-waves melted,
that gift-throne of Geats. To the good old man
sad in heart, 'twas heaviest sorrow.
The sage assumed that his sovran God
he had angered, breaking ancient law,
and embittered the Lord. His breast within
with black thoughts welled, as his wont was never.
The folk's own fastness that fiery dragon

with flame had destroyed, and the stronghold all
washed by waves; but the warlike king,
prince of the Weders, plotted vengeance.
Warriors'-bulwark, he bade them work
all of iron -- the earl's commander --
a war-shield wondrous: well he knew
that forest-wood against fire were worthless,
linden could aid not. -- Atheling brave,
he was fated to finish this fleeting life,*
his days on earth, and the dragon with him,
though long it had watched o'er the wealth of the hoard! --
Shame he reckoned it, sharer-of-rings,
to follow the flyer-afar with a host,
a broad-flung band; nor the battle feared he,
nor deemed he dreadful the dragon's warring,
its vigor and valor: ventures desperate
he had passed a-plenty, and perils of war,
contest-crash, since, conqueror proud,
Hrothgar's hall he had wholly purged,
and in grapple had killed the kin of Grendel,
loathsome breed! Not least was that
of hand-to-hand fights where Hygelac fell,
when the ruler of Geats in rush of battle,
lord of his folk, in the Frisian land,
son of Hrethel, by sword-draughts died,
by brands down-beaten. Thence Beowulf fled
through strength of himself and his swimming power,
though alone, and his arms were laden with thirty
coats of mail, when he came to the sea!
Nor yet might Hetwaras† haughtily boast
their craft of contest, who carried against him
shields to the fight: but few escaped
from strife with the hero to seek their homes!
Then swam over ocean Ecgtheow's son

....

* Literally "loan-days," days loaned to man.

† Chattuarii, a tribe that dwelt along the Rhine, and took part in
repelling the raid of (Hygelac) Chocilaicus.

lonely and sorrowful, seeking his land,
where Hygd made him offer of hoard and realm,
rings and royal-seat, reckoning naught
the strength of her son to save their kingdom
from hostile hordes, after Hygelac's death.
No sooner for this could the stricken ones
in any wise move that atheling's mind
over young Heardred's head as lord
and ruler of all the realm to be:
yet the hero upheld him with helpful words,
aided in honor, till, older grown,
he wielded the Weder-Geats. -- Wandering exiles
sought him o'er seas, the sons of Ohtere,
who had spurned the sway of the Scylfings'-helmet,
the bravest and best that broke the rings,
in Swedish land, of the sea-kings' line,
haughty hero.* Hence Heardred's end.
For shelter he gave them, sword-death came,
the blade's fell blow, to bairn of Hygelac;
but the son of Ongentheow sought again
house and home when Heardred fell,
leaving Beowulf lord of Geats
and gift-seat's master. -- A good king he!

XXXII

THE fall of his lord he was fain to requite
in after days; and to Eadgils he proved
friend to the friendless, and forces sent
over the sea to the son of Ohtere,
weapons and warriors: well repaid he

....
* Onla, son of Ongentheow, who pursues his two nephews
Eanmund and Eadgils to Heardred's court, where they have taken
refuge after their unsuccessful rebellion. In the fighting Heardred
is killed.

those care-paths cold when the king he slew.[*]
Thus safe through struggles the son of Ecgtheow
had passed a plenty, through perils dire,
with daring deeds, till this day was come
that doomed him now with the dragon to strive.
With comrades eleven the lord of Geats
swollen in rage went seeking the dragon.
He had heard whence all the harm arose
and the killing of clansmen; that cup of price
on the lap of the lord had been laid by the finder.
In the throng was this one thirteenth man,
starter of all the strife and ill,
care-laden captive; cringing thence
forced and reluctant, he led them on
till he came in ken of that cavern-hall,
the barrow delved near billowy surges,
flood of ocean. Within 'twas full
of wire-gold and jewels; a jealous warden,
warrior trusty, the treasures held,
lurked in his lair. Not light the task
of entrance for any of earth-born men!
Sat on the headland the hero king,
spake words of hail to his hearth-companions,
gold-friend of Geats. All gloomy his soul,
wavering, death-bound. Wyrd full nigh
stood ready to greet the gray-haired man,
to seize his soul-hoard, sunder apart
life and body. Not long would be
the warrior's spirit enwound with flesh.
Beowulf spake, the bairn of Ecgtheow: --
"Through store of struggles I strove in youth,
mighty feuds; I mind them all.
I was seven years old when the sovran of rings,
friend-of-his-folk, from my father took me,

....

* That is, Beowulf supports Eadgils against Onela, who is slain by
Eadgils in revenge for the "care-paths" of exile into which Onela
forced him.

had me, and held me, Hrethel the king,
with food and fee, faithful in kinship.
Ne'er, while I lived there, he loathlier found me,
bairn in the burg, than his birthright sons,
Herebeald and Haethcyn and Hygelac mine.
For the eldest of these, by unmeet chance,
by kinsman's deed, was the death-bed strewn,
when Haethcyn killed him with horny bow,
his own dear liege laid low with an arrow,
missed the mark and his mate shot down,
one brother the other, with bloody shaft.
A feeless fight,* and a fearful sin,
horror to Hrethel; yet, hard as it was,
unavenged must the atheling die!
Too awful it is for an aged man
to bide and bear, that his bairn so young
rides on the gallows. A rime he makes,
sorrow-song for his son there hanging
as rapture of ravens; no rescue now
can come from the old, disabled man!
Still is he minded, as morning breaks,
of the heir gone elsewhere;† another he hopes not
he will bide to see his burg within
as ward for his wealth, now the one has found
doom of death that the deed incurred.
Forlorn he looks on the lodge of his son,
wine-hall waste and wind-swept chambers
reft of revel. The rider sleepeth,
the hero, far-hidden;‡ no harp resounds,
in the courts no wassail, as once was heard.

XXXIII
....

* That is, the king could claim no wergild, or man-price, from one
son for the killing of the other.

† Usual euphemism for death.

‡ Sc. in the grave.

"THEN he goes to his chamber, a grief-song chants
alone for his lost. Too large all seems,
homestead and house. So the helmet-of-Weders
hid in his heart for Herebeald
waves of woe. No way could he take
to avenge on the slayer slaughter so foul;
nor e'en could he harass that hero at all
with loathing deed, though he loved him not.
And so for the sorrow his soul endured,
men's gladness he gave up and God's light chose.
Lands and cities he left his sons
(as the wealthy do) when he went from earth.
There was strife and struggle 'twixt Swede and Geat
o'er the width of waters; war arose,
hard battle-horror, when Hrethel died,
and Ongentheow's offspring grew
strife-keen, bold, nor brooked o'er the seas
pact of peace, but pushed their hosts
to harass in hatred by Hreosnabeorh.
Men of my folk for that feud had vengeance,
for woful war ('tis widely known),
though one of them bought it with blood of his heart,
a bargain hard: for Haethcyn proved
fatal that fray, for the first-of-Geats.
At morn, I heard, was the murderer killed
by kinsman for kinsman,* with clash of sword,
when Ongentheow met Eofor there.
Wide split the war-helm: wan he fell,
hoary Scylfing; the hand that smote him
of feud was mindful, nor flinched from the death-blow.
-- "For all that he† gave me, my gleaming sword

....

* Eofor for Wulf. -- The immediate provocation for Eofor in
killing "the hoary Scylfing," Ongentheow, is that the latter has just
struck Wulf down; but the king, Haethcyn, is also avenged by the
blow. See the detailed description below.

† Hygelac.

repaid him at war, -- such power I wielded, --
for lordly treasure: with land he entrusted me,
homestead and house. He had no need
from Swedish realm, or from Spear-Dane folk,
or from men of the Gifths, to get him help, --
some warrior worse for wage to buy!
Ever I fought in the front of all,
sole to the fore; and so shall I fight
while I bide in life and this blade shall last
that early and late hath loyal proved
since for my doughtiness Daeghrefn fell,
slain by my hand, the Hugas' champion.
Nor fared he thence to the Frisian king
with the booty back, and breast-adornments;
but, slain in struggle, that standard-bearer
fell, atheling brave. Not with blade was he slain,
but his bones were broken by brawny gripe,
his heart-waves stilled. -- The sword-edge now,
hard blade and my hand, for the hoard shall strive."
Beowulf spake, and a battle-vow made
his last of all: "I have lived through many
wars in my youth; now once again,
old folk-defender, feud will I seek,
do doughty deeds, if the dark destroyer
forth from his cavern come to fight me!"
Then hailed he the helmeted heroes all,
for the last time greeting his liegemen dear,
comrades of war: "I should carry no weapon,
no sword to the serpent, if sure I knew
how, with such enemy, else my vows
I could gain as I did in Grendel's day.
But fire in this fight I must fear me now,
and poisonous breath; so I bring with me
breastplate and board.* From the barrow's keeper
no footbreadth flee I. One fight shall end
our war by the wall, as Wyrd allots,

....
* Shield.

all mankind's master. My mood is bold
but forbears to boast o'er this battling-flyer.
-- Now abide by the barrow, ye breastplate-mailed,
ye heroes in harness, which of us twain
better from battle-rush bear his wounds.
Wait ye the finish. The fight is not yours,
nor meet for any but me alone
to measure might with this monster here
and play the hero. Hardily I
shall win that wealth, or war shall seize,
cruel killing, your king and lord!"
Up stood then with shield the sturdy champion,
stayed by the strength of his single manhood,
and hardy 'neath helmet his harness bore
under cleft of the cliffs: no coward's path!
Soon spied by the wall that warrior chief,
survivor of many a victory-field
where foemen fought with furious clashings,
an arch of stone; and within, a stream
that broke from the barrow. The brooklet's wave
was hot with fire. The hoard that way
he never could hope unharmed to near,
or endure those deeps,* for the dragon's flame.
Then let from his breast, for he burst with rage,
the Weder-Geat prince a word outgo;
stormed the stark-heart; stern went ringing
and clear his cry 'neath the cliff-rocks gray.
The hoard-guard heard a human voice;
his rage was enkindled. No respite now
for pact of peace! The poison-breath
of that foul worm first came forth from the cave,
hot reek-of-fight: the rocks resounded.
Stout by the stone-way his shield he raised,
lord of the Geats, against the loathed-one;
while with courage keen that coiled foe
came seeking strife. The sturdy king
....
* The hollow passage.

had drawn his sword, not dull of edge,
heirloom old; and each of the two
felt fear of his foe, though fierce their mood.
Stoutly stood with his shield high-raised
the warrior king, as the worm now coiled
together amain: the mailed-one waited.
Now, spire by spire, fast sped and glided
that blazing serpent. The shield protected,
soul and body a shorter while
for the hero-king than his heart desired,
could his will have wielded the welcome respite
but once in his life! But Wyrd denied it,
and victory's honors. -- His arm he lifted
lord of the Geats, the grim foe smote
with atheling's heirloom. Its edge was turned
brown blade, on the bone, and bit more feebly
than its noble master had need of then
in his baleful stress. -- Then the barrow's keeper
waxed full wild for that weighty blow,
cast deadly flames; wide drove and far
those vicious fires. No victor's glory
the Geats' lord boasted; his brand had failed,
naked in battle, as never it should,
excellent iron! -- 'Twas no easy path
that Ecgtheow's honored heir must tread
over the plain to the place of the foe;
for against his will he must win a home
elsewhere far, as must all men, leaving
this lapsing life! -- Not long it was
ere those champions grimly closed again.
The hoard-guard was heartened; high heaved his breast
once more; and by peril was pressed again,
enfolded in flames, the folk-commander!
Nor yet about him his band of comrades,
sons of athelings, armed stood
with warlike front: to the woods they bent them,
their lives to save. But the soul of one

with care was cumbered. Kinship true
can never be marred in a noble mind!

XXXIV

WIGLAF his name was, Weohstan's son,
linden-thane loved, the lord of Scylfings,
Aelfhere's kinsman. His king he now saw
with heat under helmet hard oppressed.
He minded the prizes his prince had given him,
wealthy seat of the Waegmunding line,
and folk-rights that his father owned
Not long he lingered. The linden yellow,
his shield, he seized; the old sword he drew: --
as heirloom of Eanmund earth-dwellers knew it,
who was slain by the sword-edge, son of Ohtere,
friendless exile, erst in fray
killed by Weohstan, who won for his kin
brown-bright helmet, breastplate ringed,
old sword of Eotens, Onela's gift,
weeds of war of the warrior-thane,
battle-gear brave: though a brother's child
had been felled, the feud was unfelt by Onela.*
For winters this war-gear Weohstan kept,
breastplate and board, till his bairn had grown
earlship to earn as the old sire did:
then he gave him, mid Geats, the gear of battle,
portion huge, when he passed from life,
fared aged forth. For the first time now
with his leader-lord the liegeman young
was bidden to share the shock of battle.
Neither softened his soul, nor the sire's bequest

....
* That is, although Eanmund was brother's son to Onela, the slay-
ing of the former by Weohstan is not felt as cause of feud, and is
rewarded by gift of the slain man's weapons.

weakened in war.* So the worm found out
when once in fight the foes had met!
Wiglaf spake, -- and his words were sage;
sad in spirit, he said to his comrades: --
"I remember the time, when mead we took,
what promise we made to this prince of ours
in the banquet-hall, to our breaker-of-rings,
for gear of combat to give him requital,
for hard-sword and helmet, if hap should bring
stress of this sort! Himself who chose us
from all his army to aid him now,
urged us to glory, and gave these treasures,
because he counted us keen with the spear
and hardy 'neath helm, though this hero-work
our leader hoped unhelped and alone
to finish for us, -- folk-defender
who hath got him glory greater than all men
for daring deeds! Now the day is come
that our noble master has need of the might
of warriors stout. Let us stride along
the hero to help while the heat is about him
glowing and grim! For God is my witness
I am far more fain the fire should seize
along with my lord these limbs of mine!†
Unsuiting it seems our shields to bear
homeward hence, save here we essay
to fell the foe and defend the life
of the Weders' lord. I wot 'twere shame
on the law of our land if alone the king
out of Geatish warriors woe endured
and sank in the struggle! My sword and helmet,

* Both Wiglaf and the sword did their duty. -- The following is
one of the classic passages for illustrating the comitatus as the
most conspicuous Germanic institution, and its underlying sense
of duty, based partly on the idea of loyalty and partly on the prac-
tical basis of benefits received and repaid.

† Sc. "than to bide safely here," -- a common figure of incomplete
comparison.

breastplate and board, for us both shall serve!"
Through slaughter-reek strode he to succor his chieftain,
his battle-helm bore, and brief words spake: --
"Beowulf dearest, do all bravely,
as in youthful days of yore thou vowedst
that while life should last thou wouldst let no wise
thy glory droop! Now, great in deeds,
atheling steadfast, with all thy strength
shield thy life! I will stand to help thee."
At the words the worm came once again,
murderous monster mad with rage,
with fire-billows flaming, its foes to seek,
the hated men. In heat-waves burned
that board* to the boss, and the breastplate failed
to shelter at all the spear-thane young.
Yet quickly under his kinsman's shield
went eager the earl, since his own was now
all burned by the blaze. The bold king again
had mind of his glory: with might his glaive
was driven into the dragon's head, --
blow nerved by hate. But Naegling† was shivered,
broken in battle was Beowulf's sword,
old and gray. 'Twas granted him not
that ever the edge of iron at all
could help him at strife: too strong was his hand,
so the tale is told, and he tried too far
with strength of stroke all swords he wielded,
though sturdy their steel: they steaded him nought.
Then for the third time thought on its feud
that folk-destroyer, fire-dread dragon,
and rushed on the hero, where room allowed,
battle-grim, burning; its bitter teeth
closcd on his neck, and covered him
with waves of blood from his breast that welled.
....

* Wiglaf's wooden shield.

† Gering would translate "kinsman of the nail," as both are made
of iron.

XXXV

'TWAS now, men say, in his sovran's need
that the earl made known his noble strain,
craft and keenness and courage enduring.
Heedless of harm, though his hand was burned,
hardy-hearted, he helped his kinsman.
A little lower the loathsome beast
he smote with sword; his steel drove in
bright and burnished; that blaze began
to lose and lessen. At last the king
wielded his wits again, war-knife drew,
a biting blade by his breastplate hanging,
and the Weders'-helm smote that worm asunder,
felled the foe, flung forth its life.
So had they killed it, kinsmen both,
athelings twain: thus an earl should be
in danger's day! -- Of deeds of valor
this conqueror's-hour of the king was last,
of his work in the world. The wound began,
which that dragon-of-earth had erst inflicted,
to swell and smart; and soon he found
in his breast was boiling, baleful and deep,
pain of poison. The prince walked on,
wise in his thought, to the wall of rock;
then sat, and stared at the structure of giants,
where arch of stone and steadfast column
upheld forever that hall in earth.
Yet here must the hand of the henchman peerless
lave with water his winsome lord,
the king and conqueror covered with blood,
with struggle spent, and unspan his helmet.
Beowulf spake in spite of his hurt,
his mortal wound; full well he knew
his portion now was past and gone

of earthly bliss, and all had fled
of his file of days, and death was near:
"I would fain bestow on son of mine
this gear of war, were given me now
that any heir should after me come
of my proper blood. This people I ruled
fifty winters. No folk-king was there,
none at all, of the neighboring clans
who war would wage me with 'warriors'-friends'*
and threat me with horrors. At home I bided
what fate might come, and I cared for mine own;
feuds I sought not, nor falsely swore
ever on oath. For all these things,
though fatally wounded, fain am I!
From the Ruler-of-Man no wrath shall seize me,
when life from my frame must flee away,
for killing of kinsmen! Now quickly go
and gaze on that hoard 'neath the hoary rock,
Wiglaf loved, now the worm lies low,
sleeps, heart-sore, of his spoil bereaved.
And fare in haste. I would fain behold
the gorgeous heirlooms, golden store,
have joy in the jewels and gems, lay down
softlier for sight of this splendid hoard
my life and the lordship I long have held."

XXXVI

I HAVE heard that swiftly the son of Weohstan
at wish and word of his wounded king, --
war-sick warrior, -- woven mail-coat,
battle-sark, bore 'neath the barrow's roof.
Then the clansman keen, of conquest proud,
passing the seat,† saw store of jewels
....
* That is, swords.

† Where Beowulf lay.

and glistening gold the ground along;
by the wall were marvels, and many a vessel
in the den of the dragon, the dawn-flier old:
unburnished bowls of bygone men
reft of richness; rusty helms
of the olden age; and arm-rings many
wondrously woven. -- Such wealth of gold,
booty from barrow, can burden with pride
each human wight: let him hide it who will! --
His glance too fell on a gold-wove banner
high o'er the hoard, of handiwork noblest,
brilliantly broidered; so bright its gleam,
all the earth-floor he easily saw
and viewed all these vessels. No vestige now
was seen of the serpent: the sword had ta'en him.
Then, I heard, the hill of its hoard was reft,
old work of giants, by one alone;
he burdened his bosom with beakers and plate
at his own good will, and the ensign took,
brightest of beacons. -- The blade of his lord
-- its edge was iron -- had injured deep
one that guarded the golden hoard
many a year and its murder-fire
spread hot round the barrow in horror-billows
at midnight hour, till it met its doom.
Hasted the herald, the hoard so spurred him
his track to retrace; he was troubled by doubt,
high-souled hero, if haply he'd find
alive, where he left him, the lord of Weders,
weakening fast by the wall of the cave.
So he carried the load. His lord and king
he found all bleeding, famous chief
at the lapse of life. The liegeman again
plashed him with water, till point of word
broke through the breast-hoard. Beowulf spake,
sage and sad, as he stared at the gold. --
"For the gold and treasure, to God my thanks,

to the Wielder-of-Wonders, with words I say,
for what I behold, to Heaven's Lord,
for the grace that I give such gifts to my folk
or ever the day of my death be run!
Now I've bartered here for booty of treasure
the last of my life, so look ye well
to the needs of my land! No longer I tarry.
A barrow bid ye the battle-fanned raise
for my ashes. 'Twill shine by the shore of the flood,
to folk of mine memorial fair
on Hrones Headland high uplifted,
that ocean-wanderers oft may hail
Beowulf's Barrow, as back from far
they drive their keels o'er the darkling wave."
From his neck he unclasped the collar of gold,
valorous king, to his vassal gave it
with bright-gold helmet, breastplate, and ring,
to the youthful thane: bade him use them in joy.
"Thou art end and remnant of all our race
the Waegmunding name. For Wyrd hath swept them,
all my line, to the land of doom,
earls in their glory: I after them go."
This word was the last which the wise old man
harbored in heart ere hot death-waves
of balefire he chose. From his bosom fled
his soul to seek the saints' reward.

XXXVII

IT was heavy hap for that hero young
on his lord beloved to look and find him
lying on earth with life at end,
sorrowful sight. But the slayer too,
awful earth-dragon, empty of breath,
lay felled in fight, nor, fain of its treasure,
could the writhing monster rule it more.

For edges of iron had ended its days,
hard and battle-sharp, hammers' leaving;*
and that flier-afar had fallen to ground
hushed by its hurt, its hoard all near,
no longer lusty aloft to whirl
at midnight, making its merriment seen,
proud of its prizes: prone it sank
by the handiwork of the hero-king.
Forsooth among folk but few achieve,
-- though sturdy and strong, as stories tell me,
and never so daring in deed of valor, --
the perilous breath of a poison-foe
to brave, and to rush on the ring-board hall,
whenever his watch the warden keeps
bold in the barrow. Beowulf paid
the price of death for that precious hoard;
and each of the foes had found the end
of this fleeting life.
Befell erelong
that the laggards in war the wood had left,
trothbreakers, cowards, ten together,
fearing before to flourish a spear
in the sore distress of their sovran lord.
Now in their shame their shields they carried,
armor of fight, where the old man lay;
and they gazed on Wiglaf. Wearied he sat
at his sovran's shoulder, shieldsman good,
to wake him with water.† Nowise it availed.
Though well he wished it, in world no more
could he barrier life for that leader-of-battles
nor baffle the will of all-wielding God.
Doom of the Lord was law o'er the deeds
of every man, as it is to-day.
Grim was the answer, easy to get,
from the youth for those that had yielded to fear!
....

* What had been left or made by the hammer; well-forged.

† Trying to revive him.

Wiglaf spake, the son of Weohstan, --
mournful he looked on those men unloved: --
"Who sooth will speak, can say indeed
that the ruler who gave you golden rings
and the harness of war in which ye stand
-- for he at ale-bench often-times
bestowed on hall-folk helm and breastplate,
lord to liegemen, the likeliest gear
which near of far he could find to give, --
threw away and wasted these weeds of battle,
on men who failed when the foemen came!
Not at all could the king of his comrades-in-arms
venture to vaunt, though the Victory-Wielder,
God, gave him grace that he got revenge
sole with his sword in stress and need.
To rescue his life, 'twas little that I
could serve him in struggle; yet shift I made
(hopeless it seemed) to help my kinsman.
Its strength ever waned, when with weapon I struck
that fatal foe, and the fire less strongly
flowed from its head. -- Too few the heroes
in throe of contest that thronged to our king!
Now gift of treasure and girding of sword,
joy of the house and home-delight
shall fail your folk; his freehold-land
every clansman within your kin
shall lose and leave, when lords high-born
hear afar of that flight of yours,
a fameless deed. Yea, death is better
for liegemen all than a life of shame!"

XXXVIII

THAT battle-toil bade he at burg to announce,
at the fort on the cliff, where, full of sorrow,
all the morning earls had sat,

daring shieldsmen, in doubt of twain:
would they wail as dead, or welcome home,
their lord beloved? Little* kept back
of the tidings new, but told them all,
the herald that up the headland rode. --
"Now the willing-giver to Weder folk
in death-bed lies; the Lord of Geats
on the slaughter-bed sleeps by the serpent's deed!
And beside him is stretched that slayer-of-men
with knife-wounds sick:† no sword availed
on the awesome thing in any wise
to work a wound. There Wiglaf sitteth,
Weohstan's bairn, by Beowulf's side,
the living earl by the other dead,
and heavy of heart a head-watch‡ keeps
o'er friend and foe. -- Now our folk may look
for waging of war when once unhidden
to Frisian and Frank the fall of the king
is spread afar. -- The strife began
when hot on the Hugas§ Hygelac fell
and fared with his fleet to the Frisian land.
Him there the Hetwaras humbled in war,
plied with such prowess their power o'erwhelming
that the bold-in-battle bowed beneath it
and fell in fight. To his friends no wise
could that earl give treasure! And ever since
the Merowings' favor has failed us wholly.
Nor aught expect I of peace and faith
from Swedish folk. 'Twas spread afar
how Ongentheow reft at Ravenswood
Haethcyn Hrethling of hope and life,
when the folk of Geats for the first time sought
in wanton pride the Warlike-Scylfings.
....

* Nothing.

† Dead.

‡ Death-watch, guard of honor, "lyke-wake."

§ A name for the Franks.

Soon the sage old sire* of Ohtere,
ancient and awful, gave answering blow;
the sea-king† he slew, and his spouse redeemed,
his good wife rescued, though robbed of her gold,
mother of Ohtere and Onela.
Then he followed his foes, who fled before him
sore beset and stole their way,
bereft of a ruler, to Ravenswood.
With his host he besieged there what swords had left,
the weary and wounded; woes he threatened
the whole night through to that hard-pressed throng:
some with the morrow his sword should kill,
some should go to the gallows-tree
for rapture of ravens. But rescue came
with dawn of day for those desperate men
when they heard the horn of Hygelac sound,
tones of his trumpet; the trusty king
had followed their trail with faithful band.

XXXIX

"THE bloody swath of Swedes and Geats
and the storm of their strife, were seen afar,
how folk against folk the fight had wakened.
The ancient king with his atheling band
sought his citadel, sorrowing much:
Ongentheow earl went up to his burg.
He had tested Hygelac's hardihood,
the proud one's prowess, would prove it no longer,
defied no more those fighting-wanderers
nor hoped from the seamen to save his hoard,
his bairn and his bride: so he bent him again,
old, to his earth-walls. Yet after him came
with slaughter for Swedes the standards of Hygelac
....

* Ongentheow.

† Haethcyn.

o'er peaceful plains in pride advancing,
till Hrethelings fought in the fenced town.[*]
Then Ongentheow with edge of sword,
the hoary-bearded, was held at bay,
and the folk-king there was forced to suffer
Eofor's anger. In ire, at the king
Wulf Wonreding with weapon struck;
and the chieftain's blood, for that blow, in streams
flowed 'neath his hair. No fear felt he,
stout old Scylfing, but straightway repaid
in better bargain that bitter stroke
and faced his foe with fell intent.
Nor swift enough was the son of Wonred
answer to render the aged chief;
too soon on his head the helm was cloven;
blood-bedecked he bowed to earth,
and fell adown; not doomed was he yet,
and well he waxed, though the wound was sore.
Then the hardy Hygelac-thane,[†]
when his brother fell, with broad brand smote,
giants' sword crashing through giants'-helm
across the shield-wall: sank the king,
his folk's old herdsman, fatally hurt.
There were many to bind the brother's wounds
and lift him, fast as fate allowed
his people to wield the place-of-war.
But Eofor took from Ongentheow,
earl from other, the iron-breastplate,
hard sword hilted, and helmet too,
and the hoar-chief's harness to Hygelac carried,
who took the trappings, and truly promised
rich fee 'mid folk, -- and fulfilled it so.
For that grim strife gave the Geatish lord,
....

* The line may mean: till Hrethelings stormed on the hedged
shields, -- i.e. the shield-wall or hedge of defensive war -- Hrethe-
lings, of course, are Geats.

† Eofor, brother to Wulf Wonreding.

Hrethel's offspring, when home he came,
to Eofor and Wulf a wealth of treasure,
Each of them had a hundred thousand*
in land and linked rings; nor at less price reckoned
mid-earth men such mighty deeds!
And to Eofor he gave his only daughter
in pledge of grace, the pride of his home.
"Such is the feud, the foeman's rage,
death-hate of men: so I deem it sure
that the Swedish folk will seek us home
for this fall of their friends, the fighting-Scylfings,
when once they learn that our warrior leader
lifeless lies, who land and hoard
ever defended from all his foes,
furthered his folk's weal, finished his course
a hardy hero. -- Now haste is best,
that we go to gaze on our Geatish lord,
and bear the bountiful breaker-of-rings
to the funeral pyre. No fragments merely
shall burn with the warrior. Wealth of jewels,
gold untold and gained in terror,
treasure at last with his life obtained,
all of that booty the brands shall take,
fire shall eat it. No earl must carry
memorial jewel. No maiden fair
shall wreathe her neck with noble ring:
nay, sad in spirit and shorn of her gold,
oft shall she pass o'er paths of exile
now our lord all laughter has laid aside,
all mirth and revel. Many a spear
morning-cold shall be clasped amain,
lifted aloft; nor shall lilt of harp
those warriors wake; but the wan-hued raven,
fain o'er the fallen, his feast shall praise
and boast to the eagle how bravely he ate
when he and the wolf were wasting the slain."
....
* Sc. "value in" hides and the weight of the gold.

So he told his sorrowful tidings,
and little* he lied, the loyal man
of word or of work. The warriors rose;
sad, they climbed to the Cliff-of-Eagles,
went, welling with tears, the wonder to view.
Found on the sand there, stretched at rest,
their lifeless lord, who had lavished rings
of old upon them. Ending-day
had dawned on the doughty-one; death had seized
in woful slaughter the Weders' king.
There saw they, besides, the strangest being,
loathsome, lying their leader near,
prone on the field. The fiery dragon,
fearful fiend, with flame was scorched.
Reckoned by feet, it was fifty measures
in length as it lay. Aloft erewhile
it had revelled by night, and anon come back,
seeking its den; now in death's sure clutch
it had come to the end of its earth-hall joys.
By it there stood the stoups and jars;
dishes lay there, and dear-decked swords
eaten with rust, as, on earth's lap resting,
a thousand winters they waited there.
For all that heritage huge, that gold
of bygone men, was bound by a spell,†
so the treasure-hall could be touched by none
of human kind, -- save that Heaven's King,
God himself, might give whom he would,
Helper of Heroes, the hoard to open, --
even such a man as seemed to him meet.

XL

....

* Not at all.

† Laid on it when it was put in the barrow. This spell, or in our
days the "curse," either prevented discovery or brought dire ills on
the finder and taker.

A PERILOUS path, it proved, he[*] trod
who heinously hid, that hall within,
wealth under wall! Its watcher had killed
one of a few,[†] and the feud was avenged
in woful fashion. Wondrous seems it,
what manner a man of might and valor
oft ends his life, when the earl no longer
in mead-hall may live with loving friends.
So Beowulf, when that barrow's warden
he sought, and the struggle; himself knew not
in what wise he should wend from the world at last.
For[‡] princes potent, who placed the gold,
with a curse to doomsday covered it deep,
so that marked with sin the man should be,
hedged with horrors, in hell-bonds fast,
racked with plagues, who should rob their hoard.
Yet no greed for gold, but the grace of heaven,
ever the king had kept in view.[§]
Wiglaf spake, the son of Weohstan: --
"At the mandate of one, oft warriors many
sorrow must suffer; and so must we.
The people's-shepherd showed not aught
of care for our counsel, king beloved!
That guardian of gold he should grapple not, urged we,
but let him lie where he long had been

....

* Probably the fugitive is meant who discovered the hoard. Ten
Brink and Gering assume that the dragon is meant. "Hid" may
well mean here "took while in hiding."

† That is "one and a few others." But Beowulf seems to be
indicated.

‡ Ten Brink points out the strongly heathen character of this part
of the epic. Beowulf's end came, so the old tradition ran, from his
unwitting interference with spell-bound treasure.

§ A hard saying, variously interpreted. In any case, it is the
somewhat clumsy effort of the Christian poet to tone down the
heathenism of his material by an edifying observation.

in his earth-hall waiting the end of the world,
the hest of heaven. -- This hoard is ours
but grievously gotten; too grim the fate
which thither carried our king and lord.
I was within there, and all I viewed,
the chambered treasure, when chance allowed me
(and my path was made in no pleasant wise)
under the earth-wall. Eager, I seized
such heap from the hoard as hands could bear
and hurriedly carried it hither back
to my liege and lord. Alive was he still,
still wielding his wits. The wise old man
spake much in his sorrow, and sent you greetings
and bade that ye build, when he breathed no more,
on the place of his balefire a barrow high,
memorial mighty. Of men was he
worthiest warrior wide earth o'er
the while he had joy of his jewels and burg.
Let us set out in haste now, the second time
to see and search this store of treasure,
these wall-hid wonders, -- the way I show you, --
where, gathered near, ye may gaze your fill
at broad-gold and rings. Let the bier, soon made,
be all in order when out we come,
our king and captain to carry thither
-- man beloved -- where long he shall bide
safe in the shelter of sovran God."
Then the bairn of Weohstan bade command,
hardy chief, to heroes many
that owned their homesteads, hither to bring
firewood from far -- o'er the folk they ruled --
for the famed-one's funeral. " Fire shall devour
and wan flames feed on the fearless warrior
who oft stood stout in the iron-shower,
when, sped from the string, a storm of arrows
shot o'er the shield-wall: the shaft held firm,
featly feathered, followed the barb."

And now the sage young son of Weohstan
seven chose of the chieftain's thanes,
the best he found that band within,
and went with these warriors, one of eight,
under hostile roof. In hand one bore
a lighted torch and led the way.
No lots they cast for keeping the hoard
when once the warriors saw it in hall,
altogether without a guardian,
lying there lost. And little they mourned
when they had hastily haled it out,
dear-bought treasure! The dragon they cast,
the worm, o'er the wall for the wave to take,
and surges swallowed that shepherd of gems.
Then the woven gold on a wain was laden --
countless quite! -- and the king was borne,
hoary hero, to Hrones-Ness.

XLI

THEN fashioned for him the folk of Geats
firm on the earth a funeral-pile,
and hung it with helmets and harness of war
and breastplates bright, as the boon he asked;
and they laid amid it the mighty chieftain,
heroes mourning their master dear.
Then on the hill that hugest of balefires
the warriors wakened. Wood-smoke rose
black over blaze, and blent was the roar
of flame with weeping (the wind was still),
till the fire had broken the frame of bones,
hot at the heart. In heavy mood
their misery moaned they, their master's death.
Wailing her woe, the widow* old,

....

* Nothing is said of Beowulf's wife in the poem, but Bugge sur-
mises that Beowulf finally accepted Hygd's offer of kingdom and

her hair upbound, for Beowulf's death
sung in her sorrow, and said full oft
she dreaded the doleful days to come,
deaths enow, and doom of battle,
and shame. -- The smoke by the sky was devoured.
The folk of the Weders fashioned there
on the headland a barrow broad and high,
by ocean-farers far descried:
in ten days' time their toil had raised it,
the battle-brave's beacon. Round brands of the pyre
a wall they built, the worthiest ever
that wit could prompt in their wisest men.
They placed in the barrow that precious booty,
the rounds and the rings they had reft erewhile,
hardy heroes, from hoard in cave, --
trusting the ground with treasure of earls,
gold in the earth, where ever it lies
useless to men as of yore it was.
Then about that barrow the battle-keen rode,
atheling-born, a band of twelve,
lament to make, to mourn their king,
chant their dirge, and their chieftain honor.
They praised his earlship, his acts of prowess
worthily witnessed: and well it is
that men their master-friend mightily laud,
heartily love, when hence he goes
from life in the body forlorn away.
Thus made their mourning the men of Geatland,
for their hero's passing his hearth-companions:
quoth that of all the kings of earth,
of men he was mildest and most beloved,
to his kin the kindest, keenest for praise.

....
hoard, and, as was usual, took her into the bargain.

Other Works Published by the East India Publishing Company

The Anglo-Saxon Chronicles
Alfred the Great

The Pirates Own Book
Charles Ellms

Adventures of a Soldier
Edward Costello

Three Months in the Southern States
Arthur Fremantle

Macbeth
William Shakespeare

King Lear
William Shakespeare

Second Treatise on Government
John Locke

The Autobiography of Benjamin Franklin
Benjamin Franklin

A Tale of Two Cities
Charles Dickens

www.eastindiapublishing.com

Made in the USA
Middletown, DE
09 June 2021